domino

Your Guide to a Stylish Home

domino

Your Guide to a Stylish Home

discovering your personal style and creating a space you love

by *domino* editors
Jessica Romm Perez
Shani Silver

Text by Nicole Sforza
Designed by Jennifer S. Muller

Produced by

MELCHER MEDIA

Published by

Simon & Schuster

Simon & Schuster
1230 Avenue of the Americas New York, NY 10020

For information about special discounts for bulk purchases, please contact
Simon & Schuster Special Sales at 1-866-506-1949 or business@simonandschuster.com

The Simon & Schuster Speakers Bureau can bring authors to your live event.
For more information or to book an event contact the Simon & Schuster Speakers Bureau
at 1-866-248-3049 or visit our website at www.simonspeakers.com

Produced by
MELCHER MEDIA 124 West 13th Street, New York, NY 10011
www.melcher.com

Printed in China
10 9 8 7 6 5 4 3 2 1

Library of Congress Cataloging-in-Publication Data

Title: Domino : your guide to a stylish home / editors of Domino,
Jessica Romm Perez, Shani Silver.
Other titles: Domino (Simon and Schuster, Inc.) | Domino
(Condé Nast Publications)
Description: First Simon & Schuster hardcover edition. | New York:
Simon & Schuster, 2016.
Identifiers: LCCN 2016031819 (print) | LCCN 2016032162 (ebook)
| ISBN 9781501151873 (hardcover) | ISBN 9781501151880 (ebook)
Subjects: LCSH: Interior decoration.
Classification: LCC NK1990 .D66 2016 (print) | LCC NK1990 (ebook)
| DDC 747--dc23
LC record available at https://lccn.loc.gov/2016031819

ISBN 978-1-5011-5187-3
ISBN 978-1-5011-5188-0 (ebook)

Cover art: Timorous Beasties wallpaper pattern "Butterflies"
timorousbeasties.com

to the dedicated readers of *domino*—then, now, and always.

CONTENTS

INTRODUCTION

In our first book, *domino: the book of decorating*, you welcomed us into your space as we defined the essentials that make a home complete. Here, in our second book, we'll find out what makes a home yours.

We couldn't be happier to be home with you again, helping you discover your personal style. We will go beyond basics and show you how style comes to life in a room, and throughout a home. In the pages that follow, we'll walk with you through the design moments that define your personal style, and we'll help you bring them home.

We'll share rooms we love, statement-making ideas to guide and inspire you, side-by-side examples that illuminate ideas, and our favorite home decor finds (and where to shop for them). We'll meet trusted voices in style and interiors who will share their advice on how to create the best space for you. Through it all, you'll find exciting inspiration and design solutions that are relatable, motivating, and above all, brimming with style.

It's good to be home, again. Welcome to *domino*.

Your Editors,

Jessica Romm Perez + Shani Silver

1
OWN YOUR STYLE

Design success comes down to being confident in your choices. So many people decorate for others—they're concerned about outside opinions and wanting to impress. But you don't live in a hotel. You're not decorating for the gala of the century. It's your home, and it should feel like a home— with character and imperfection and all the things that make you happy.

Your home needn't be pristine and poised, as if you're trying to win an award. It should be a place you live your life the way you want. If you can't confidently entertain in your dining room, or relax with a good read in a favorite chair, how can you feel at home? What makes a home great—and great for you—is when it feels like you. And that's our goal here—to help you personalize your surroundings, often with items you already own, so that when you walk through the door, you feel an instant sense of welcome, calm, and home.

A brazen mix of color, pattern, and art expresses the creative nature of the homeowner.

1 get inspired

It's tough to style a space if you don't know what your style is, but there are ways to find your design voice. Zero in on what inspires you. The amount of information out there is overwhelming, but you can use it to your advantage. Scour Pinterest, steal ideas from a favorite restaurant, and start to build inspiration boards. Follow people on Instagram whose style you admire. Check out fashion designers, artists, architects, and gardening gurus.

If you're a hands-on type, great—grab a bulletin board and get to work; use anything from a cool embossed coaster to a fabric swatch in a color you're obsessed with. Tear out magazine pages of rooms that feel right, pin up paint chips, and include pictures of places that speak to you—the woods, the desert, distant destinations—then find images of furnishings that evoke the same feelings. You'll start to see themes developing— colors you're drawn to, pieces that feel right.

Practice gleaning inspiration from your everyday life, too. Look at the places you frequent through a new lens. Maybe you've always admired the light fixture in your favorite coffee shop—ask where it's from. During movie marathons, pay attention to interior scenes and note any items that stand out to you. When you go to someone's house, think about what you like and what you'd change; pinpointing what you don't love helps you identify what you do.

When your home truly starts to resemble you—the clothes you'd wear, the accessories you'd choose—you know you're onto something. It makes sense—your home is an extension of you, an embodiment of your personality. If you're a black, gray, and navy person, with nary a pattern to be seen, maybe that bold print sofa isn't the right fit. If you gravitate toward chunky sweaters, perhaps a slouchy, deep armchair is your thing and you can skip the angular version. So peek into your closet for inspiration.

A wood-paneled wall helps unify a bevy of inspiration and turn it into a point of interest. Mixing clippings with a mobile, necklace, plant, and tapestry sparks imagination and fosters a free-spirited feel.

2 find your aesthetic

Identifying the styles you like is a key component of crafting a home that feels like you.

Maybe you're into modern, clean lines and livable, simple furnishings. If too much stuff stresses you out and you like things with clear function, you may lean more toward minimalism or airy, fresh Scandinavian style. Perhaps you're a flea-market aficionado who spends all day foraging for treasures. Or you're a midcentury fan and the sight of an iconic molded plastic chair or elegant teak bar cart excites you. If you're a go-with-the-flow type who can't be bound by rules—preferring distressed furniture to polished pieces, intricate patterns to blocks of color—then you're more bohemian.

Homebodies and outdoorsy types are often drawn to a rustic style—with comfy sofas, lived-in furniture, weathered wood, and an earthy palette. Traditional types appreciate history, familiarity, and warmth. Some people like to showcase things that others want to hide—piping, bulbs, ducts—and prefer an industrial look.

You don't have to pick one look and stick with it. You can mix things up, pairing a brass sconce with a dhurrie rug. But knowing what excites you helps define your style. Those tough decisions will become few and farther between, because if you've figured out what you like, you'll make decorating decisions from a more relaxed, confident place. And every piece will contribute to making your home a comfortable haven.

3 take action

It's tough to infuse your space with fresh energy when old items bring you down. Furnishings emit a sort of energy, too—so if a chair looks sad and you're just not feeling it, maybe it isn't meant for your space.

Walk around your home with notebook in hand and your go-to style(s) in mind; look at each item and decide if you love it. If you're not into something, let it go; you'll be able to replace it with something you adore. Indecision is stagnation, and making one decision can open the floodgates for others to follow. The more decisions you make, the more confident you'll become.

Group items that make the cut by texture, color, material, and size, so you can see how they work together. And take note of what you need to buy. When it's time to get working, break projects into manageable chunks. Write a to-do list, and be specific: Go to a paint store; test samples; ask friends for painter recommendations; and so on. Maybe you take on one project a weekend, but start small— empty a bookshelf and fill it up with things you love to see when you enter the room.

Commit to creating a home that truly reflects who you are. Push yourself. Typically, the decorating decisions that feel a little bit scary at first are the ones you'll end up cherishing the most.

As you push forward, keep in mind that a personality-packed home:

sparks stories: Meaningful objects—whether an heirloom quilt or a photo blown up from vacation—tell a story about who you are and give people insights into your character. They signal that your home is more about the people within it than the actual furnishings.

evolves over time: People change, tastes change, situations change—and so should your home. Objects are added to vignettes and replaced, photos are swapped out, paint colors evolve.

plays with contrast: Opposing forces give a home a sense of push-and-pull. Black with white, rough with smooth, tall with short, modern with traditional—these are the types of pairings that make a space feel alive.

has rhythm: A home should have an almost perceivable pulse—a certain energy you feel right when you walk inside, a sense of movement that's created from thoughtfully placed patterns, rooms that flow into the next, a color palette that ushers you from room to room.

takes risks: Truly memorable rooms don't always play it safe. A huge painting as a focal point, a moody sculpture, a wooden floor painted an unexpected color all signal that your space is an expression of you with special attributes that no one else can claim as their own. When you can infuse a home with personality and warmth, that's when you've made styling magic.

The best displays aren't just for show—they evoke emotion. Weave in a few of your most intimate personal possessions for maximum impact.

4 let it flow

It's important to note that your home will never truly be "done"—and it never has to be. It's understandable to want to feel like a project is finished, but your style will evolve, and your home will be an expression of that. When we're so focused on the outcome, we don't enjoy the process (as much). When you see your space as an ongoing project, great things can happen—and stress won't weigh you down. Sometimes when you least expect it,

rather than when you're actively looking, a mirror or console that's perfect will come into your life. Be patient and wait to find pieces that inspire you.

Your home isn't simply the items in it—it is more about crafting a space to share with the people you love. It doesn't need to be perfect—it just needs to be perfect for *you*.

Weaving in treasures and artifacts from world travels allows your home to grow with you, turning it into a living, breathing interpretation of your life.

Curvy chairs mimic the lines of a midcentury table, while beadboard walls add textural contrast.

2

SEATING

SEATING
WE LOVE

smart ideas for every
room in the house

office

Swap out a standard desk chair for one with style to spare and
you'll change the whole feel of the room. Plush padding promises
comfort, a solid wood frame guarantees stability, and the small
scale is perfectly proportioned for a space-challenged alcove.

entryway

A rustic wooden bench is welcoming and provides a
place to slip on shoes. Art makes an often neglected
spot feel like a real room.

dining room

Thanks to vibrant green paint, traditional chairs shed their formality and add an element of personal style and boldness. The chairs' spindles echo the vertical lines of the ample windows.

living room

A spacious living room can handle multiple layers of seating, from a comfy couch to deep armchairs to lightweight occasional chairs that can move around with ease. The lipstick-red legs on an Eames wire chair offer a colorful diversion within a neutral scheme.

bedroom

Happiness is a chocolate velvet love seat at the foot of a canopy bed. The settee's small scale adds comfort to the room without overpowering it.

dressing room

Seating should suit the space: In a cool, unexpected nook, a blue stool feels at home among colorful shoes and bags. The hue complements the wallpaper and art, and the texture adds a layered element that completes the corner.

HANDBOOK

understanding upholstery

		why we love it	*take note*
leather		Like a moto jacket, it's tough, cool and luxe, and can handle the occasional spill.	Shinier versions will feel cold on bare skin—have lots of throws on hand.
wool		Durable and soft, plus it's naturally wrinkle- and pill-resistant.	Look for a wool blend for more stain resistance and less chance of felting (where fibers rub together to form felt).
silk		It doesn't get more chic than this. A silk settee? Count us in.	Silk isn't hardy enough for your everyday sofa; it needs professional cleaning if stained.
linen		Crisp and slightly textured, it's an elegant choice that won't fade or pill.	Linen stains and wrinkles easily, and can weaken when exposed to too much sun.
cotton		It can go formal (damask) or casual (canvas). Cotton velvet is sumptuous yet surprisingly durable—the perfect mix.	Dirt and dust will show and so will wrinkles, but blending cotton with other materials makes up for these shortcomings.
synthetics (olefin, acrylic, polyester, rayon, acetate, nylon)		On their own, blended together, or blended with natural fibers, these fabulous options win on many fronts— most are wrinkle-, stain-, and fade-resistant.	Acetate (imitation silk) is still delicate, so, like true silk, it's best for a showpiece not everyday seating.

STYLE STATEMENTS

snapshots of inspiring ideas

minimalist

the mood: clean, unencumbered, graphic.

styling notes: Finding a sectional big enough for this loft-like space was difficult, so three twin mattresses were framed in plywood instead; the lids along the arms and back flip up to reveal storage. Furthering the low-lying scheme, the coffee table is actually two Ikea TV stands with the legs removed.

classic

the mood: fresh, elegant, cheerful.

styling notes: In a formal room, sunny yellow upholstery feels like a welcome relief, whisking away potential stuffiness and fostering a friendly vibe. The detailing on the chair frames echoes the textured, paneled walls.

eclectic

the mood: unconventional, collected, fun.

styling notes: Solid upholstery and white walls allow the rest of the room to wave its flag (literally). Geometric patterns, from the tiled fireplace to the pillows, are big and bold—small prints would feel too busy in this bustling space.

get the look

midcentury

A lounge-worthy dining set and matching wood floors bring the high ceilings and elaborate 19th-century moldings down to earth. With no upholstery in the room, subtle bursts of color from a cobalt sculpture and orange floor lamp add warmth and energy.

saucer pendant

oval dining table

Ellsworth Kelly monograph

burnished vase

plywood chair

sheepskin rug

marble arch candleholder

Turn to page 270 for information on these products.

STYLE SCHOOL

a few of our favorite chairs

2. the rocking chair

Exciting in both material (lacquered steel slung with leather) and color, this rocker is the brainchild of Belgian husband-and-wife team Hannes Van Severen and Fien Muller. It's a brilliant example of marrying function with flair.

1. the acapulco

Pear-shaped and cushion-free, it brings beach vibes a bit of cool structure. The steel frame is wrapped with comfy vinyl cord that won't get hot in the sun, easily hoses down, and never stays wet.

3. the modern wingback

When you want to shut out the world but still be comfortable, it doesn't get better than a chair with generous proportions and a sense of exclusivity. A wingback looks particularly throne-like at the head and foot of a dining table and pairs well with a large sofa and roaring fire, too. This version, designed by Luca Nichetto, features layered, upholstered panels resting on a solid wood base.

4. the bergère

This stately lounging chair, with an exposed wooden frame, upholstered back, and loose seat cushion, dates to 18th-century France. It blends seamlessly into a French country style, but can also hold its own in an eclectic space, bringing a refined air.

5. the paimio

A stunning example of midcentury prowess, Alvar Aalto's 1932 design is made of a bent birch frame with a thin plywood seat that scrolls at the top and bottom for resiliency. The back reclines slightly for comfort, and two side loops act as chair arms, legs, and floor runners.

6. the bertoia diamond

Designed in 1952, this iconic beauty is a fluid, almost aerodynamic wonder crafted of welded mesh steel that's strong but airy. It manages to be delicate and industrial at the same time.

7. the modern slipper

Introduced in 18th-century Europe, these petite, armless, often low-to-the-ground chairs allowed women wearing layers upon layers of clothing to more easily put on their slippers. Today's tailored, more streamlined silhouettes take over where full-size chairs can't go, such as an awkward corner, a landing, or at the foot of a bed. This plush version pairs a raffia base with linen upholstery.

perfect perches

pouf

frequently spotted...
as a footstool in the living room;
as an extra seat in a packed family
room; or in a kids' room as an
all-purpose activity perch.

specs
These laid-back loungers are
typically 16 to 22 inches in diameter
and about 12 to 17 inches high.

materials
Treat a pouf as an accent piece—
think cool metallics, sleek cowhide,
chunky knits, or the irresistible
softness of Mongolian lamb fur.

ottoman

frequently spotted...
placed in pairs in the living room or at the end of your bed; in the kids' room doing double duty as a desk chair and toy chest—storage versions are clutch.

specs
Roughly the same height as your sofa looks best. Top with a tray and it's a table—just leave a few inches of space all around so you still have room to prop your feet.

materials
Look for hardy materials like leather, indoor/outdoor fabric, or a washable slipcover. And don't go matchy-matchy here—contrast the sofa and use a wild pattern, lots of tufting, piping, or nailhead trim. X-bases add geometry.

bench

frequently spotted...
in the entryway; at the foot of a bed; on one side of a kitchen or dining table to maximize seating and add variety.

specs
Many benches are 18 to 20 inches tall; to ensure two people will fit comfortably, go for at least 48 inches long.

materials
Crushed velvet or silk are fantastic for a piece that doesn't get too much use, and don't overlook outdoor pieces—metal or wood in a fun color can look incredible inside, especially topped with a cushion. If the bench is against the wall, forgo a back (it's airier).

style standoff

symmetry vs. asymmetry

symmetry: Logical, ordered setups suit those craving balance and serenity. Try this if you have a focal point to decorate around, such as a fireplace or built-in bookcases. Keep some things askew, so it doesn't feel contrived. Here, throw pillows share a palette, but their designs differ slightly; same with the art. One floor lamp off to the side prevents the room from feeling too prim.

asymmetry: Unstructured seating feels playful and casual, and instantly puts people at ease. The arrangement allows for more flexibility, giving you freedom to arrange and rearrange on a whim, and to work in one-of-a-kind flea-market finds when inspiration strikes.

style standoff

patterned sofas vs. solid sofas

patterned: Bold prints inject energy, and can happily hide spills and marks. A neutral pattern (this is Brunschwig & Fils' Les Touches) lets you toss in colorful accents and change them at will. Play around with contrast; try a modern print on a traditional sofa, or a sweet floral on a straight-lined couch.

solid: One-note upholstery feels soothing and calm. When paired with a matching rug, you've got a pleasant, muted canvas for introducing pattern elsewhere. A statement wallpaper wall behind the sofa feels fresh.

pattern party

complementary colors

Orange and blue are across from each other on the color wheel, so the sofa and art intrinsically balance each other. And the value (or vividness) of both colors is similar. Covering a traditional sofa with an electric color feels fresh, as does the all-over pillow parade. Though the pillows are various sizes and patterns, they mesh well because they all feature blue, orange, black, or white.

big and small prints

Patterns on opposite sides of the style spectrum (a buttoned-up pinstripe and a free-spirited floral) can play nice as long as they share a similar tone. And everybody has a palette pal—the green floral chairs speak to the fiddle-leaf fig tree, the pink and purple rug to the flowers, and the black-and-white settee to the lamp shade, table base, and dresser.

bonnie's tips

1. Keep it all very natural. I call it "orderly chaos." For example: Instead of putting your collection of cups in one straight line across a shelf, stack them at different heights or put them on top of plate stacks in various colors and textures. It's more interesting to style your home in such a way that is not completely perfect.

2. Use natural light when photographing moments in your house. If necessary, put things near a window to help maximize the daylight.

3. Try to keep the background as neutral as possible, especially if the foreground has a lot going on. Also, be careful to avoid too much clutter when taking a "shelfie" or photographing a vignette. Keep it simple and well-balanced.

4. Make it a true expression of yourself.

5. Don't post randomly. Photograph moments that feel special, and choose the right time to share them. Make sure you are complementing your overall feed, so there's a sense of continuity.

6. Stick to a unified palette when buying special objects. Staying true to the colors that express your personality will not only make for a stronger feed, it will also help define your own personal style.

inspiring style:

bonnie tsang
(on the art of photo sharing)

Originally a graphic designer, Bonnie Tsang took an unusual road to becoming a photographer. While embracing motherhood and with plenty of encouragement from her photographer father, she began documenting her new life with her young child. Her snapshots attracted a large audience. "I started posting pictures of my daughter on Flickr (the social media du jour at the time). Luckily for me photographs of kids happen to be extremely popular and I began to build a real following."

"As a photographer, I love anything that helps me get my ideas out into the world. In the old days, we would just share with our immediate circle of friends, but now—with blogs, Instagram, and Pinterest—there's a huge audience." Photographs might feature anything from a beautiful breakfast she has created, to a still life of her bedside table, to some newly purchased bed linens. "If the lighting is perfect and the messiness is just right, it makes me want to pick up my camera or phone and snap a picture to share with the world."

3 no-fail seating setups

formal

A squared-off, elegant look, with two chairs facing the sofa, parallel to each other, and a small table in between, makes for a balanced look that has depth.

something in between

Two chairs facing the sofa but angled toward each other creates a circular, familial feel with no corners to bump into—great with a round coffee table.

playing with height: low-lying seating

Relaxed, inviting, and the epitome of casual-chic, a low-lying arrangement (about 33 or 34 inches high) can make a tight space feel bigger and low ceilings feel taller. The look can be well-traveled and formal or bohemian and fun; either way it'll have a gather-round-and-chat-all-night feel, especially when joined by floor cushions (and a wood-burning fireplace, preferably of the midcentury variety). Use floor-hugging coffee and side tables, so the look feels consistent and it's not awkward to grab a drink or switch on a light; tables should line up with your sofa cushions or be about 2 inches below. Include one or two "regular" height chairs in the mix to accommodate people who might be uncomfortable going low. For a more traditional take on a lower seating option, try an English sofa.

casual
An L-shaped design gives everyone lots of space to stretch out. Sectionals are perfect for a laid-back look.

(btw)

In a very large room, you'll want to get creative with seating arrangements to make sure the space doesn't feel empty. Pull furniture off the walls for a cozier feel (walls left bare can take a console with ottomans underneath and a mirror above, or a floor-to-ceiling art treatment). And bring in extra seating to delineate space: Chaises, daybeds, and benches work well because they're easy to see over. Consider carving out a reading nook in a corner with an armchair and an ottoman. Or bring in a small table and two chairs that you can use for writing, playing games, and dinner for two.

seating arrangement suggestions

effortless flow
Keep pathways clear so one has a sense of being ushered into the space. You don't want to step over an ottoman or scoot around a too-big side table to get to the main seating area.

a sense of containment
Use a rug to ground the area and make it feel cozy and inclusive.

sofa sidekicks
Rounded coffee tables are friendly and never look crooked. Square and rectangular tables feel orderly.

room to breathe
The coffee table should be far enough from seating that you don't have to shimmy through, but not too far that you have to strain to grab a drink. About 18 inches away is the sweet spot.

separate zones
In a large room, consider placing sofas or chairs back-to-back (shown left) to carve out two distinct seating areas. Screens, shelves, or large plants can be used to fill space or soften corners.

a chair buffet
Vary your seating options to appeal to the masses. Think deep armchairs for reading, smaller upright chairs for conversing or working, maybe a few comfy floor pillows too. Just pay attention to balance: You don't want a huge hulking sofa opposite two airy Bertoia chairs—the room will feel lopsided.

conversation starters
Intriguing sculpture, artsy books, or photos tucked under a glass-topped table all give guests something to talk about.

an inspiring view
Face a chair to take in the scenery. Use mirrors to reflect pretty items if outside views are limited.

inspiring style:

aurora james
(on statement chairs)

Aurora James, founder and creative director of Brother Vellies, works with artisans from all over the world to create traditional African footwear with her own added flair. Her fashion sense, honed by extensive travel in Africa, has given her an eye for interior design.

When it comes to seating, Aurora loves a chair that makes a statement: "It's my passion! Essentially the chair is the island of the room, and it can make a big impact. It dictates the way you hold yourself: For example, a cozy rocking chair where you can lounge and rock holds a body very differently than a hard wooden stool does. Chairs decide how you are physically interacting with a room—the energy of that space, and how the room's inhabitants are going to communicate."

Aurora's personal favorites are her beloved Milo Baughman chairs. She found them on Craigslist and they stole her heart. "At any one time I'm on the lookout for twenty different things on my wish list, and they always have a way of finding me."

aurora's tips

1. Upholstering is a great way to keep things modern and feeling new. Don't be afraid of it. Start with something small, like a stool, that's not a huge commitment financially or emotionally and see how it goes. The process is fun and quite addictive.

2. Look for a vintage chair that has an interesting shape—one that sparks your imagination. Introducing older pieces into a contemporary environment changes the space by adding a layer of history and depth.

3. Nothing has to be perfect. Let your chair be a work-in-progress. One of my pieces, which is upholstered in indigo and old denim, is always being patched and worked on. The flaws have become the chair's story. For me, these are the elements that turn a house into a home.

4. Think long and hard about the colors! It's nice to have something a little surprising and unexpected. Use the chair to make a personal bold statement.

5. Chairs don't always need to have their feet on the ground. I also love my rattan chair that swings from the ceiling.

DIY wall decals, made from cut strips of black gaffer tape, electrify an entry and dictate the room's palette.

3
WALLS

WALLS
WE LOVE

smart ideas for every
room in the house

bathroom

An intricate tile pattern
takes an architecturally
uninspiring bathroom to
the next level. The ornate
Venetian mirror echoes
the curves of the tiles,
while modern sconces and
a sleek faucet ensure the
look doesn't veer too far
into old-world territory.
An open console sink
allows the tile to make an
uninterrupted statement
throughout the room.

bedroom

This enchanting botanical wallpaper is almost transportive, making climbing into bed a true escape. Patterned pillows bring the colors of the wallpaper to the forefront, and a macrame hanging adds a personal touch that makes the room feel lived in. The wallpaper stops short of the ceiling, creating a cozy headboard-upon-headboard effect.

kids' room
Chalkboard paint inspires
creativity, guarantees
an ever-changing art
installation, and even
looks good when messy.
Furnishings in muted,
chalky hues blend
effortlessly.

nook

Sometimes you just need to go for it: The powerful wallpaper print, the bold color choice. You're creating a space that makes you happy—rather than following an imagined rule book. Every unique aspect of this nook suggests it was thoughtfully composed, and is loved.

HANDBOOK

paint
your walls

types of paint

Focus on oil-based or water-based. Water-based paint is so saturated and high quality (not to mention mild in odor and fast-drying) it's the most common choice. Oil-based paint is often used for a super-smooth, super high-gloss look on woodwork or doors.

flattering finish

When in doubt, go matte or flat, which doesn't have any shine. Its velvety texture hides minor flaws, absorbs light, touches up easily, and always looks polished. Eggshell, which has a slight sheen and stands up well to moisture, is a good choice for kitchens and bathrooms, but just make sure you're okay with the shine level—some versions may be shinier than your preference. Semi-gloss works well on trim, and allows you to easily swipe smudges from shoes or strollers. Hi-gloss or lacquer can be stunning when you want drama—consider it for a powder room.

to prime or not to prime?

Sometimes a separate primer is truly necessary: When walls are badly stained or damaged (sand any peeling parts first) or when you're painting a light color over a dark color. If your walls are in good shape, opt for a paint-and-primer combination. Swipe walls with a damp cloth first to get rid of surface dust and ensure the paint will cling.

how much to buy?

Figure 1 gallon for every 350 square feet. (Get a general idea by adding up the length of all walls, multiplying by the ceiling height, then dividing that number by 350.) Err on the generous side: You'll want extra paint for touch-ups, and buying a new batch at another time may result in a slightly different color.

mix and match

If you're set on a color from one paint company but love the coverage and consistency of another, ask the paint or hardware store if they'll mix the formula of the first company in the base of the second (many will).

testing

A paint color won't look the same on your walls as it does in the store, at your friend's house, or even in the can. That's because light affects the colors we see—so the same color may look very different throughout the day and may vary based on the light bulbs you choose. Paint a section of wall with a color you're considering. Choose an eye-level spot, and ideally one that can be seen from another room. Peek at the color morning, noon, and night—with the lights on and the lights off—before committing.

weather watch

Rain and humidity may lead to drips and delayed drying times, so choose a dry day.

insurance against mishaps

Create a touch-up kit—pour leftover paint into a jar labeled with the color name and room you used it in.

fun with wallpaper

	why we love it	*take note*
marbled	Organic and mesmerizing, it can feel cool or warm, depending on the colors and pattern.	Striking in the bathroom as a clever twist on traditional marble. Just look for vinyl or non-woven papers, which can handle moisture.
flocked	Velvety, raised designs feel at once playful and glamorous, and hide wall imperfections effortlessly.	Be forewarned: You'll definitely have guests pawing your paper. The textured sections may show dust.
woodgrain	From surprisingly realistic roughcut firewood to cartoon-like planks; adding warmth with wood will forever be cool.	This has the most impact in unexpected places: Try a washed-out woodgrain in a nursery or an indigo version in a powder room.
grasscloth	Tasteful texture might be exactly what's missing from a space.	The material is very delicate, and seams are nearly impossible to conceal; you'll have to live with them as part of the design.
metallic	Fabulous, light-reflective foil can make a small room bigger and a dark room lighter. It's also steam-resistant and easy to clean.	It's fragile, so needs to be installed with care. And since it's thin, it'll show every little lump and bump—only use on clean, pristine walls.

types of wallpaper

pre-pasted
Glue embedded into the paper is activated with a wet sponge.

paste-the-wall
Glue is applied directly to the wall. It's the least mess going up, but trickiest to remove.

peel-and-stick
Like contact paper, the back gets peeled off and up it goes. Designs are limited, though.

where to hang wallpaper

Any room can benefit from wallpaper, whether it's a subtle tactile grasscloth in a hallway (shown right) or an eye-popping, 3D hit for the office (shown opposite). Even the kitchen can be wallpapered without feeling overwhelming. Wallpapering all four walls in a room is a statement for sure, especially if you cover the ceiling for a jewel-box effect. But a focal wall can have just as much impact. When doing one wall, pull out a color from the wallpaper to paint the remaining walls. And save ultra-crazy patterns for behind or next to the sofa, bed, or desk, so you can appreciate the pattern when you walk in without being distracted by it the entire time you're in the room.

(btw)

hire it out

Wallpapering is a specialized skill, with lots of cutting and measurements involved, so we strongly suggest calling a pro. Ask friends and family for recommendations, or tap a local hardware store.

STYLE STATEMENTS

snapshots of inspiring ideas

whimsical

the mood: energizing, fantastical, fun.

styling notes: An animated palm tree print matches the eclecticism of the ephemera resting in front, from vintage glassware and golden pears to a throwback record player and a ceramic pig.

modern

the mood: serene, straight-lined, refreshing.

styling notes: This abstract wallpaper's horizontal stripes stretch out the small powder room; the open vanity and glass shelf keep things airy. Handsome details—a leather mirror, rough-hewn wide-plank floors—are juxtaposed with delicate frosted-glass sconces and fluffy white towels for soothing balance.

bold

the mood: quirky, old-school, opulent.

styling notes: Pink walls (Benjamin Moore's Cinco de Mayo), a technicolor Persian rug, vintage art, and proper fittings give this foyer eclectic but demure charm. Though the 1876 house could have been done up in a more subdued style, the marriage of bohemian and preppy touches makes it unforgettable.

romantic

the mood: picturesque, cheerful, sweet.

styling notes: Deliciously dreamlike de Gournay wallpaper makes it feel like you're being whisked to a faraway land without the flight. With a backdrop this gorgeous, furnishings are kept minimal, so as not to distract from the poetic print.

get the look

rustic

White wood-paneled walls, a painted brick backsplash, and cabinets made of reclaimed lumber transform a cabin kitchen into a study in textures and contrast. Marble countertops feel cool, roman shades bring in warmth. Pairing different tones of white keeps the look from feeling sterile.

oil decanter

covered serving dish

traditional rolling pins

glass + leather decanter

wooden trencher board

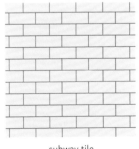

Shaker-inspired chair

copper measuring cups

subway tile

Turn to page 270 for information on these products.

STYLE
SCHOOL

dark walls

There's no reason to be afraid of the dark—at least when it comes to paint. Moody walls instantly ground a room and up its cool quotient. They also mask imperfections, like uneven walls, and create the illusion of infinite space. These five tricks ensure your space skews more daringly dramatic than dreary dungeon.

1. **Blasts of color** act as a welcome respite from the intensity of the hue.

2. **White accents** pop against dark walls. Here, the ceilings, trim, window treatments, and oversize pendant all offer crisp contrast.

3. **Reflective elements** like the porthole-like mirrors, chrome table base, and brass chair legs bounce light around the room.

4. **Traditional details**, such as the carved wooden armoire, pastel oil painting, and mahogany floors, keep the room from feeling stark.

5. **Big art** goes a long way, covering up a large expanse of the dark wall to define the space.

white walls

White paint is often thought of as a throwaway, an almost too-easy default—but it can be the trickiest color of them all. Some whites have sneaky chameleon-like tints; others feel so bright they'll make you squint. Consider:

undertones

When shopping around, look at the fan deck to see if the white leads to an orangey color (then it's warm) or a blue or purplish color (then it's cool). Hold paint chips next to a sheet of white paper to judge their true hue. Complement the tones already in the room. If you have lots of warm colors, try whites with warm undertones (red, yellow, pink, orange). If cool colors abound, consider cool whites (with undertones of blue, green, or purple). If you feel uneasy about going decidedly warm or cool, opt for a balanced white in the middle.

warm whites

These feel comforting and enveloping, complementing neutral tones and pairing nicely with wooden accents and floors (shown right). They also work well with ultra-traditional styles—especially creamy, antique whites that give off a lived-in, been-around-the-block feel.

cool whites

Sometimes cool whites come off as new and crisp—but they can also veer toward cold. Pairing with brass accents adds warmth (shown far right). Cool whites tend to work well in modern spaces and with riotous color. Grayish white is a go-to backdrop for art—many galleries employ gray walls as they make the colors of artwork stand out.

natural light

If your room gets lots of natural light, a warm white may make it feel even warmer, sometimes too warm. Compensating with a cool white will lower the temperature a bit. If you don't have many windows and rely on artificial light, a warm white will cozy up the room.

style standoff

large patterns vs. small patterns

Both large and small patterns act as instant style definers—an in-your-face abstract graphic
screams modern; a wispy floral leans more traditional but can still hold its own in an eclectic space.

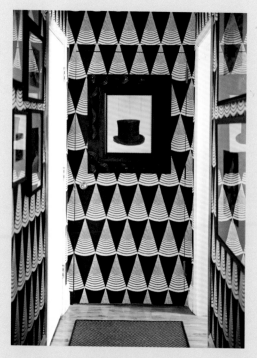

Large patterns steal the show and allow
furnishings to remain minimal. In a wallpapered
hallway, hanging art in the same colorway is a no-fail
way to make a small space feel cohesive; in a bedroom,
wallpapering behind the bed allows you to forgo a
headboard. Large-scale patterns, especially in rich,
dark colors, can make a big room feel more intimate
and a small space feel more important.

Small patterns add depth and texture from afar,
and tell a story up close. They run the gamut from
charming and whimsical to wild and dizzying, so
bring home samples to test out the look. A tiny, airy
print in a pale color can make a space feel bigger; a
dense print in a dark, warm color can make it feel cozy.

pattern effects

A print with movement is the easiest way to invigorate a blank wall. Think zigzags for a shot of energy, florals for a romantic vibe. To add a sense of structure to rooms in need of a focal point, consider a grid that immediately commands attention. Wallpapering all four walls can foster the impression of continuous space.

For an intriguing take on texture, try faux bois or marbleized paper, or paper that mimics stone. A botanical is a smart visual trick in rooms with no views.

In a cavernous space, create intimacy by installing a chair rail and wallpapering below.

The way a wallpaper pattern runs can also help define a space:

horizontal patterns make a room feel wider.

vertical patterns make a room seem taller, especially with ceilings painted white.

diagonal patterns (shown left), called drop patterns, add rhythm and work well if walls and ceilings are uneven—they'll mask imperfections by drawing the eye from corner to corner.

ceilings with character

rustic canopy

Raw wood beams give a serene living room tactile charm and a warm sense of structure. Contrasted against the earthy ceiling stripes, a starburst fixture feels even more otherworldly.

5 ways to treat a ceiling

1. classic
Paint the ceiling white for crisp contrast against colorful walls.

2. enveloping
Match the walls for the effect of being cradled in color.

3. tonal
Go slightly darker or lighter than the walls for a subtle surprise that feels comfortable.

4. bold
Paint the ceiling a completely different color than the walls (think pale pink above, olive all around).

5. cherry on top
Cover the ceiling in a fun color and keep the walls white. Perfect in a space that craves an unexpected moment.

golden glow
A metallic ceiling acts like flickering candlelight in a traditional room, adding warmth, sparkle, and shine (which tricks the eye into thinking the ceiling is taller).

room-to-room views

Always take surrounding spaces into consideration so that there's a sense of flow and continuity. Think of your home as one big palette, rather than separate rooms with distinct colorways.

colors as a bridge
Choose a hue to showcase in all rooms, even if tones vary. A hallway wallpapered in a sunny yellow floral can lead to an office with cream-painted walls, as shown here.

similar shades
If you have dark paint in one room, add white to the can to create a complementary color in an adjacent room. Or look to the paint deck and choose a color on the same card.

furnishings that play along
Use a color from the rug, upholstery, or window treatments in one room as the paint color for another. If you paint two nearby rooms drastically different colors, try rugs that feature each of those colors to help connect the rooms.

common denominators
Keep the color of baseboards, moldings, and door and window frames consistent throughout the home. Repeating accessories from room to room, like white picture frames or one green potted plant, fosters a sense of community.

remedies
for renters

1. Two-tone walls are a smart trick for when you can't adjust the architecture; painting the bottom half high-gloss black helps ground the space, and feels like an unexpected choice for a beach house. Forgo multiple nail holes by clipping art to twine with binder clips, then casually lean some art as well (shown top left).

2. If you're not thrilled about the paint color your landlord chose but don't want to repaint, use wallhangings with abandon—they'll cover up large swaths of wall and add texture and character (shown top right).

3. A curtain can divide a room while adding a layer of softness. White feels fresh and ethereal, like a natural extension of the walls (shown bottom).

window frames

black magic
Painting frames the same glossy black as kitchen cabinetry creates graphic simplicity. Greenery seems almost neon in contrast, and the white ceiling, floor, backsplash, and pendants shed some light on the darkness. Bonus: Pitch-black muntins disappear at night.

monochromatic minimalism
Crisp white surfaces keep a small room from feeling cramped—the eye is immediately drawn to a lush green view just outside.

gutsy contrast
Pulling out a color from the
floor tiles makes window
frames an integral part of
the design, and negates the
need for window treatments.

inspiring style:

barbara bestor

(on color + paint)

Architect Barbara Bestor designs contemporary environments for everyday life by staying true to her manifesto: "Everyone should experience strange beauty every day." "I had a real breakthrough years ago in using color," Barbara explains. "I was building a house for myself and my young girls. I wanted to reflect their interests in my plans. They loved pink and magenta and reds and the clash of colors in that spectrum."

That house, in Echo Park, California, was where Barbara developed not only her signature saturated accent colors but also the dark blue/black paint that she often uses for her exteriors.

Barbara frequently employs a subdued backdrop and uses strong colors as highlights: bright floor tiles, faucets, cabinet doors, closets, and light fixtures. "Bathroom fixtures are a fun place to use bright colors. If everything else in a room is white, a really cool, brilliantly colored faucet makes it surprising. If you have white or light gray walls, the color can come from furniture and light fixtures. The accent pieces become showstoppers."

Another technique she uses is to "dunk" a room in a solid paint color from top to bottom—including the trim—for an immersive effect. "I guess the big difference is that I use color from an architect's point of view, adding it as a way to replace a material. Perhaps a client can't afford to put in wood floors? A solution might be to do a linoleum floor in bright colors."

1. Let yourself go crazy with color in the small rooms—like laundry rooms and pantries. These are great places to be bold. Acid green, yellow, or magenta walls with simple white shelves to offset the color will give you a rush of pleasure every time you open the door.

2. Doors are a great way to introduce color into a room. Black and navy or dark gray are nice alternatives to the usual white or wood. Just be careful to paint the door the same color on both sides, so it won't seem half done; and be sure the door color is in harmony with the colors inside the room as well as outside. Use top-quality enamel paint for both the interior and exterior doors. It's worth spending the extra money for rich color that won't fade.

3. A good rule of thumb is that anything that will have fingers touching it should be painted in at least a semi-gloss for easy maintenance. Everything else should be in matte paint. If there are little kids in the house, try a racing stripe of the gloss version of the matte wall paint (from the ground up to about three feet high). It will look great and is easy to keep clean.

4. If your ceiling is in decent shape, paint it with a high-gloss white paint. It essentially acts as an illuminator and fills the room with a magical light.

5. Create interesting features by painting floors or wooden staircases or using colorful floor tiles.

Crisp white art pops against an inky blue wall and speaks to the shape of the console.

4

ART

ART
WE LOVE

smart ideas for every
room in the house

bedroom

Hung corner to corner, a
fringe-laden handwoven
hammock, discovered on a
trip to Tulum, Mexico, spans
the room and billows in the
breeze, eliminating the need
for a headboard.

dining room

A framed grizzly bear photo adds texture, softening the white-painted brick wall and mirroring the richness of the dark ceiling. One big piece rather than a series of smaller ones feels confident and calm.

kids' room

3D art feels appropriate in a spot fit for wild imaginations. Even the Ikea bed flaunts a creative hack thanks to added floral wallpaper that matches the adjacent wall.

kitchen

When a sink doesn't have a view, create one with art.
A grouping of oil paintings gives the room a time-worn
sense of history. Plants and antlers on the wall and
counter push the boundaries of the arrangement.

entryway

A perfectly imperfect floor-to-ceiling gallery wall evokes controlled chaos. One larger artwork anchors the mix of frames—some left empty, others filled with mementos. Sticking to white mats and limiting the frames to gold, white, and black gives the wall a soothing sense of purpose, even with an excess of art.

HANDBOOK

art ideas

consider

old photos
Framed shots of relatives or even yourself as a child feel soulful and special.

graphic posters
When framed simply, pieces from artists like Rothko, Warhol, and Picasso look timeless.

sketches
Even a simple pencil sketch can feel like a treasure.

your own shots
Blow them up to roughly 30 x 40 inches.

black-and-white photography
You can't go wrong. It's sleek, it's graphic, and even inexpensive versions can look high-end.

where to look

flea markets
They are the perfect places to gather unusual pieces.

art galleries
Photographs and prints are typically the cheapest, but you don't have to buy anything. Just notice what you're drawn to—maybe it's seaside scenes or modern city life.

student art shows
A general rule: Stick to abstracts and graphic paintings rather than portraiture.

museum shops
If you like a particular exhibit, snag a poster or print from the show.

places far from home
Vacations are a great way to score meaningful, one-of-a-kind finds. Anything from tapestries by local artisans to photos or sculpture will remind you of your trip for years to come.

(btw)

Not sure where to start? Match the mood. Choose art in a similar style to your room, and all will be well. A casual space will look great with well-worn flea-market frames. A fancy, glam interior? Not so much.

mats
+ frames

mats

Go neutral here; white, cream, or pale gray showcases art without overpowering it. Fabric mats (linen/canvas) lend softness and texture and feel like a natural match for traditional landscapes.

frames

Custom frames can cost double or even triple what you paid for your print. Try:

thin black or white
The safest choice, easily lending a minimalist touch. Works well with posters, photography, and prints.

sleek silver
Elegant with a crisp white mat and bold, abstract art.

wood
A wonderful way to add warmth. Use simple birch frames for a clean, modern vibe.

gilded
Burnished frames complement historical prints or paintings while giving abstracts (like the one above by Hugo Guinness) a touch of glamour. No need to go too ornate here—spare versions pack enough of a punch.

above a mantel

Leave 3 to 6 inches between mantel and
art. Leaning pieces works well, too.

(btw)

You don't need art on every wall. It's better to create a
few intimate groupings rather than dot the room with
pieces that don't relate.

on a furnitureless wall

Hang art about 58 inches on center
(meaning measure from the floor to the
center of the art); for a gallery wall, treat
all your pieces as one and measure to the
center of the grouping. Hanging at this
height keeps art spaced well in relation
to the other furnishings in the room, and
works whether you're standing or sitting.
Hang too high (as many people do) and
 art gets lost.

STYLE
STATEMENTS

snapshots of inspiring ideas

country

the mood: relaxing, muted, quaint.

style notes: An envelope of art around a brass bed feels like a comforting canopy. Central symmetry loosens up on the sides to prevent the grouping from feeling static. Same-color mats that tie to the pillow and blanket unify the room, as do the mostly botanical prints in muted black and gray hues.

collected

the mood: chill, flexible, simple.

styling notes: A collage-like composition. Pieces feel casual and personal—some overlap, others are clustered—for a fluid, art-project appeal. Sconces on either side give the scene a sense of structure.

linear

the mood: vibrant, fun, kaleidoscopic.

style notes: Hanging art horizontally underneath an alcove ceiling brings the focus down, creating a cozy, tight-knit nook. Bright-white walls act as a sedate backdrop for the technicolor prints—a series of studies by artist Tom Herbert—while a small lamp breaks the line of art so it's not too perfect. Geometric pillows act as small pieces of art; curvy chairs soften the squares and chunky lacquered side table.

70s

the mood: nostalgic, pure, laid-back.

style notes: Bare wood frames match the rawness of the unpainted door and feel simple and stress-free. No-fail formula: one horizontal, one vertical, and an unusual object (shown here, raccoon tails) to connect the two.

get the look

graphic

A striking, sizable piece of art above the bed makes the need for a traditional headboard feel passé. Hanging the art vertically, as well as topping a leggy side table with a skinny desk lamp, gives the room a sense of height. The art's geometric lines are echoed in the pared down bedding and throw pillow.

bright throw pillow

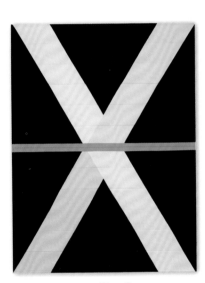

graphic quilt

bold table lamp

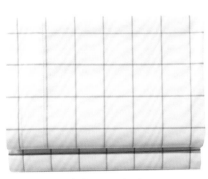

windowpane sheets

modern stool

abstract painting

Turn to page 270 for information on these products.

STYLE SCHOOL

how to hang a gallery wall

visualize it
Pick a tone you want to set and a loose palette. Some similarity among pieces is good—a shared color, theme, or size. This arrangement leans heavily on black and white, but pops of color keep it fun and tied to the furnishings.

curate it
Gather pieces in similar shapes but throw in a few contrasting objects. An oval or circle will soften all those angles. Plan for varying sizes; large art makes an impact and small art is great for filling in gaps. Go for a mix of frame colors—metal, white, black—so the cluster feels like it was acquired over time. Leaving one piece unframed is a nice touch and feels raw and painterly.

arrange it
Experiment with placement on the floor in front of the wall until the look feels balanced. Place the largest item a bit off-center so the layout feels unpredictable. Vary orientation with vertical and horizontal pieces—too many of one kind will feel stuffy.

hang it
Arranging art above a piece of furniture, like a sofa or console, balances the visual weight below. Plan for about 3 inches between frames—too close and the cluster will feel crowded, too far away and it'll feel disconnected. And use two hooks per piece for stability.

(btw)
Mixing mediums is a good thing. Prints, sketches, photos, paintings, even a child's masterpiece can all cohabitate as long as a shared color palette runs through the arrangement.

living in 3D

Sprinkling in objects, like an instrument or a metal flower, gives what would have been a flat arrangement depth, personality, and substance. Try to keep the item roughly the same size as the art so it blends in. You can even hang art around an existing wall sconce, which will shed light on your new arrangement.

big art

Large pieces command attention, anchor a room, and make an impact that a bunch of small art just can't. And the sheer scale gives a sense of wise intention, even if you're an interior design novice.

color theory

Pairing oversize art with a tiny bouquet in the same palette creates a fun juxtaposition of big and small. The art on the floor completes the scene for a triangular composition that feels casual but considered.

abstract idea

White walls and furnishings set the stage for a symmetrical blast of DIY art—a Pierre Frey fabric stretched over canvas.

natural selection

Two horizontal pieces centered on the wall, rather than the sectional, contrast vertical wall panels and elongate the space. Inspired by the surrounding landscape, the photos (by Melanie Pullen) pull together the colors of the room, while adding depth and mirroring the pair of ottomans in front.

leaning art

No measuring, no nail holes, no commitment. When done right, casually leaned displays feel cool and collected. And—bonus— they can be positioned to hide things like wall outlets and wires and will always stay level. To ensure it doesn't look like you just got too lazy to grab the hammer, cluster a bunch of art of varied heights but similar mood, or work just one piece—either massive or tiny—into a vignette so it feels like it belongs.

on ledges

Varying the space between frames makes this rotating gallery feel spontaneous. Sprinkling in small objects, like rocks found on family beach trips, allows the array to be appreciated up close. Shelves the same color as the walls fade away, keeping the focus on the art.

on the floor

A floral sketch adds life to the lower half of a room. In a serene space with minimal furnishings, everything appears sculptural.

5 more places to display art

1. on a windowsill
Scenic shots can sweeten a view.

2. above a doorway
A small piece above the molding is a treasure when you look up.

3. on a chair
Dress up an antique that's no longer a comfortable place to sit.

4. on an upright piano
An unexpected way to break up the boxiness.

5. on an artist's easel
A perfect pairing that can fill an empty corner.

in a desk

An oil painting tucked into an emerald green nook feels like part of the landscape. Layering objects in front adds dimension.

style skills:
use art to...

subdue a space

A picture of an Italian harbor helps eliminate mental clutter. The frame is similar in texture and color to the hamper, while the white mat matches the chair.

create an instant headboard

Hang a bold piece of painted linen on the wall to make a floor-bound bed feel purposeful, rather than haphazard.

add soul

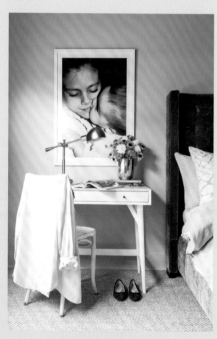

Blowing up meaningful shots feels appropriate in a bedroom.

mask an uninspiring view

lighten the mood

unify disparate pieces

Suspended from the ceiling with fishing line, a vivid print breaks up a blast of beige and distracts from a so-so view when the blinds are pulled up.

Tucking lighthearted photo strips behind a more serious oil painting (with loose photos casually placed in front) signals this is a home.

A grouping of art extends beyond the sofa to wrap around a side table, mimicking the S-shaped lamp base and creating a whole new vignette.

mirrors
as art

doubles as a window

A well-placed gilded mirror is ornate enough to serve as the dining room's main event, while cleverly reflecting smaller pieces across the way.

bathroom brightener

A 19th-century trumeau mirror moderates the starkness of a modern space with old-school grandeur.

masters of illusion

Hung in columns right up to the 14½-foot ceiling, a grouping of gilded mirrors found in flea markets accentuates a loft's scale and bounces around light.

inspiring style:

graham kostic
(on collecting + displaying)

"Art collections can seem intimidating," says Graham Kostic, creative director of the online video magazine glossedandfound.com, "so I like to keep it theatrical and a little tongue-in-cheek." Graham's passion for collecting started young. "Ever since I was a child I've been completely fascinated by souvenir shopping. On vacations I would always search for the most obscure, authentic items to bring home, where I would display them as collections."

graham's tips

1. Whether you're buying serious, collectible art as an investment, or just collecting flea market treasures, make sure each piece is inspirational, moving, and tells a good story. The joy the piece gives you should warrant the price you pay.

2. Framing something turns it into art. Try framing faded vintage postcards or black-and-white antique photographs to create unique pieces. Do the same with groupings of Polaroid pictures. Once framed and hung together, Polaroids become little mini-art collections of their own.

3. Avoid being precious about displaying art; it is not just about creating a perfect gallery wall. Mix your special things among functional items. Adding art to an open kitchen cabinet or bookshelf can elevate everyday things while giving you the joy of seeing your treasures throughout the day.

4. Creating a grouping of art is a perfect way to offset the potential imperfections of individual pieces. A collection becomes more than the sum of its parts.

5. Stand-alone art should be able to hold its own and be perfect enough to warrant a place on a mantel or coffee table.

Zebra meets chevron in this dynamic tile; two bathmats placed vertically help define double sinks (and echo the floor pattern on a smaller scale).

5
FLOORING

FLOORS
WE LOVE

smart ideas for every
room in the house

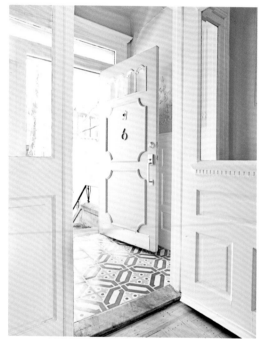

entryway

Foyers have to handle high impact. These
hand-crafted cement floor tiles have
movement and flow—perfect for ushering
people in and out of a high-traffic spot.
The design mimics the door trim, and the
punchy color, though maybe too much in a
large space, is delightful in small doses.

kitchen

Reclaimed 1920s Moroccan tiles make a simple kitchen
feel like an old soul. The colors of the midcentury chair,
country stool, industrial pendant, Moroccan screen, and
farmhouse table are all represented in the floor, which
helps the various styles to coexist.

dining room

This over-dyed flat weave radiates youthful energy, coaxing the dark floor and serious wood table to join the party.

kids' room

Sophisticated flat weaves in sweet hues are a refreshing change from primary colors. The larger rug's motif echoes the ceiling; the smaller rug defines a play zone and can be easily tossed in the wash.

living room

A pale gray mottled rug gives the effect of stone without the chill.

HANDBOOK

flooring
materials

		why we love it	*take note*
solid wood		Warm and homey, wood gets better with age, can be refinished several times, and never goes out of style.	Expands in humidity, so not great for damp areas like basements. Pre-finished wood will wear even better but cost a bit more.
engineered wood		Layering a thin veneer of real wood over plywood results in a doppelgänger that's cheaper and less susceptible to humidity.	Sometimes you can feel the difference underfoot. And you'll only be able to refinish it once, if at all.
linoleum		Made of linseed oil and wood products, it's a durable biodegradable choice infused with mineral pigments for bright, fun colors.	Look for versions with a protective coating to resist stains; otherwise, if it's in a well-trafficked area, you'll need to refinish every couple of years.
ceramic tile *(opposite page)*		The mix of clay and minerals results in a powerhouse that resists wear, water, stains, scratches, and dents—especially if glazed.	Textured or matte tiles are less slippery. Grout lines need cleaning; consider dark grout to mask dirt or matching the grout to the tiles so lines disappear.
concrete		An understated, low-maintenance choice that looks amazing and also happens to be hypoallergenic.	Choose a finish to suit your style—matte feels edgy and industrial in a kitchen; polished can be elegant in a dining room.
laminate		Layers of fiberboard with a melamine resin top mimic various materials. Easy to clean, and extremely stain- and scratch-resistant.	Laminate may trick the eye from afar, but up close it won't fool anyone. And standing water will cause damage.

rug materials

		why we love it	*take note*
wool		Super-soft, wears well, and contains natural oils that keep dirt from adhering to fibers. Plush sheepskins have become requisite bedside companions.	Wool attracts allergens, so you'll need to clean regularly with a HEPA-equipped vacuum. Some wool sheds excessively.
cotton		Casual and soft. Cotton is most often used for flat-weaves like kilims and dhurries. You'll also find cotton-wool blends that are less expensive than pure wool.	Cotton attracts dust and dirt, so it's not great in high-traffic areas. And thin ones won't last a lifetime.
naturals (sisal, jute, coir, hemp, seagrass)		Staples in decor-savvy homes, and for good reason: Woven with plant fibers, they trap dirt (great under kitchen tables!) and are strong, renewable, neutral, and beautifully textural.	They can shed, and the coarse texture isn't particularly foot-friendly—but you can layer with a soft rug on top.
indoor/outdoor		Synthetic materials like polyester and polypropylene mimic natural fibers but are extremely sturdy, fade-proof, and stain-resistant.	You're not going to be reveling in their luxurious feel—these are workhorses.

overdyed rugs

A brilliant blend of modern in-your-face color with a traditional motif, overdyeing typically involves bleaching, dyeing, and washing a rug to get a saturated stunner that has a peek of pattern. With such vibrance underfoot, it's nice to keep furnishings sedate, but that doesn't mean sacrificing texture. The white-painted brick wall, rough-hewn pedestal, and rustic wood floors add dimension.

tile sizes, shapes + patterns

Tiles run the gamut from tiny mosaics to 2 x 4 planks, and then some. Sixteen- and 18-inch squares are popular for floors, but there's a massive size range, and you'll want to consider the effect.

Large tiles can make a room feel bigger, in part because fewer grout lines means less interruption. Small tiles can feel busy and overwhelming in a big space, but in a powder room they work well. Wrapping floors and walls in the same tiny tile (shown right) can blur lines and make the room feel infinite.

To minimize grout lines, choose rectified tiles—their edges are extra precise, resulting in lines that are barely noticeable.

(btw)

The number of grout colors is endless, but caulk (which you'll need for corners, among other things) comes in just a few shades. So if you're picky about grout and caulk colors matching exactly, choose your caulk color first— then match the grout.

The way tiles are arranged has a huge effect on the feel of the space. Laying tiles diagonally can visually expand a room, making it feel wider by drawing the eye to the corners. A straight-on checkerboard feels more strict and structured. A pattern using different sizes of squares and rectangles (called a Versailles pattern) can make a room feel larger. Here, a few of our favorite shapes:

hexagon
Try a floral design, all one color, or a random mix.

subway
Typically done in one color, or various tones of the same color. Metallics and glass tiles offer a nice twist on tradition.

penny rounds
These can swing strikingly modern or charmingly classic.

squares
Try shades of one hue for calm, monochromatic for sleek, an elaborate colorful design for striking.

fish scales
Lovely, and appropriate, in a bathroom.

graphic
An intricate design fosters a global feel underfoot.

rug sizes

It's tempting to choose a rug solely on appearance, but size is crucial. A too-small rug will look like a postage stamp and make the room feel smaller. A rug that's too large, with not enough floor space around it, will feel sloppy (you'll want about 18 to 24 inches of bare floor all around). Standard rug sizes are 4 x 6, 5 x 7, 6 x 9, 8 x 10, and 11 x 14.

A large rug is great for uniting the elements of a room, and a series of smaller rugs can be used to define various seating areas. Either way, a rug shouldn't float like a lonely island in the middle of the room— at least some of your seating options should touch the rug. If you're not sure about size, use this guide: Get a rug 2 feet shorter than the walls of your room. So if your room is 10 x 12 feet, an 8 x 10 should do the trick. Here, some room-by-room tips:

dining room
Rugs here are great for buffering lively dinner conversation; just have them extend 18 inches on all sides of the table so chairs can be pulled out and remain on the rug. This wavy rug softens the linear nature of the room, from the table base's vertical bars to the angular light fixture and gridded art.

bedroom
Rough-hewn wood floors and a giant wool and sisal rug ground the bed in texture. Allowing the rug to peek out about a foot on both sides of the bed ensures a roomy enough landing pad.

hallway
Treat a wide hallway like a destination rather than a journey with rugs and furnishings, such as slim seating, intriguing artwork, and an unexpected place to hang your hat. These three geometric Moroccans play off one another, while feeling distinctly separate. To keep things airy, leave 4 to 6 inches of bare floor between the wall and the rug.

rug
shapes

Round rugs are inviting and intimate, providing a refreshing change of pace that instantly enlivens a room and softens its edges. Try them in an entryway, under a round dining table, or in any space that needs to lighten up (an office, a laundry room). Round rugs work nicely as the second rug in a room, to spotlight an area like a reading nook. Just make sure it's big enough so that some furniture can rest on it.

Runners and hallways go hand-in-hand, but also consider them for long, thin kitchens, walk-in closets, and at the sides or foot of the bed. In a bathroom, they can span the length of a double-sink vanity or a gorgeous claw foot tub. Runners are fantastic when they are thick and plush—think of them for luxury rather than just as a way to get from here to there. And since they're often in high-traffic areas, a slip-proof rug pad is a must.

STYLE STATEMENTS

snapshots of inspiring ideas

graphic

the mood: confident, bold, energizing.

styling notes: Open chairs and pale walls let a classic checkerboard floor steal the show. With such a bang underfoot, it's crucial to keep other colors and patterns to a minimum; a blue sideboard and fresh greens are the only bright hits.

beachy

the mood: weathered, casual, cozy.

styling notes: This rug's frame and border give a room with various patterns and organic elements a welcome sense of structure. Selecting a rug the same color as the floor expands the surface area of the room.

industrial

the mood: minimal, unassuming, humble.

styling notes: Though free from bells and whistles, there's something so inviting about an industrial space: Pared down to the essentials, it's not trying to be anything other than what it is. The polished stone floor gets a bit of warmth from simple wood furnishings and stacked rattan poufs.

get the look

scandinavian

A pale wide-plank floor feels fresh, while exposed knots add rustic charm to keep the look from feeling sterile. Scaled back and simple, the room's clean lines evoke a sense of peace and clutter-free serenity. Consistent colors are calming; the floor is the same color as the top of the Swedish trestle table; white Ikea chairs match the walls, window treatments, and candlesticks.

cord pendant

Swedish farmhouse table

Eames chair

beechwood utensils

Nordic dinnerware

folk candlestick tray

Turn to page 270 for information on these products.

STYLE SCHOOL

layering rugs

Like topping a blouse with a blazer, layering rugs is a finishing touch that promises a pulled-together, polished look. A layered look can highlight a specific area; add color, contrast, and texture; and allow you to use a small rug in a big space without it looking like the wrong choice.

sheepskin over stripes
Beachy meets cozy in this opposites-attract match made in heaven.

dhurrie over wool
Similar to how your favorite chambray shirt can tone down an outfit, a blue-fringed number tossed on sophisticated wool makes this office feel less Monday morning, more casual Friday.

kilim over wool

A sunny yellow topper helps a wool rug lighten up, and lines up with the sofa edge to create a precise seating area that still feels playful.

persian over jute

Casual jute tempers the too-traditional feel of a Persian, making it look rebellious rather than rule-abiding.

the white rug: do you dare?

White can be just as practical as darker colors as long as it's in the right room and you follow these guidelines.

do...
Opt for wool or synthetics—they resist stains well. And choose extra stain protection, if available.

Consider fluffy white options like sheepskins and flokatis—their long fibers trap dirt, so it's not as visible on the surface.

Pair with furnishings you really want to showcase—white is a blank canvas that allows others to shine.

Contrast textures—a high-pile rug like a shag is perfect with a sleek leather sofa; a tighter weave may suit velvet upholstery better.

Go for white if you've got a light-haired pet. You won't see fur as much.

don't...
Use white in a room that gets lots of action—entryway, family room, kids' room. Save white rugs for formal living rooms, bedrooms, guest rooms, and offices.

Trample all over your new white rug with shoes—the less grime on these guys, the better. Vacuum regularly to eliminate dirt before it gets ground in.

Get white if you're truly nervous about it. Instead, choose cream with a subtle tone-on-tone pattern. You'll get a similar effect without the stress.

style standoff

dark floors vs. light floors

Dark floors like ebony and walnut are rich and dramatic, providing visual weight below to keep furnishings grounded. And they look fantastic paired with pale walls. But dark floors may show scratches, lint, and dust.

Light floors feel effortless and airy and work with many styles, from bleached-out beachy to glossy stark modern. They can make a dark space feel lighter and a pale space even brighter by reflecting light.

style standoff

patterned rugs vs. solid rugs

Patterned rugs pull all the colors of a room together, making everything from throw pillows and vases to books feel like one big happy family. Try zigzags or stripes to push the boundaries of tight spaces; use a medallion design in rooms that crave an anchor (top with an acrylic coffee table so as not to cover the pattern).

Solid rugs act as a calming foundation, furthering the serenity of a neutral room or chilling out a space that already boasts plenty of prints. Whether you go light or dark depends on the the vibe you want; light rugs visually enlarge a room; dark rugs up the cozy factor.

painted floors

Treating floors like a canvas can take your style up a notch. Look to surrounding art and wallpaper patterns when deciding on a color; whimsical mint green floors (shown right) and pale gray trim feel like a treat. Imagine what this room would have looked like with standard wood floors—not nearly as enchanting.

remedies for renters

1. Vinyl stick-on floor tiles ease the transition from indoors to outdoors. Using an intricate pattern helps tile lines fade away, so the effect is more like a painted floor (shown top left).

2. Placing carpet tiles is an easy way to soften a space and add pattern (shown top right).

3. Top badly stained or scratched floors with a makeshift seating area propped with a throw and floor pillows to make it feel intentional (shown bottom).

inspiring style:

elsie larson

(on having fun with flooring)

Nashville based blogger, designer, and DIY queen Elsie Larson of abeautifulmess.com feels it is important to not ignore the floor. Instead, she encourages using it to make a statement.

"In our current home we took a lot of risks. I wanted to stay away from anything too heavy and serious." As a result, floors throughout her house are, for the most part, painted bright white. The exception? In a bold move, a pretty teal blue high gloss covers her living room floor, inspired by the Surf Lodge Hotel in Montauk, New York. Elsie is a big fan of using inspirational rugs to enhance rooms as well.

elsie's tips

1. Always get the largest rug you can afford. It should cover ¾ of the room. The biggest mistake people make is buying a rug too small for the room. Ideally, the rug should reach beyond all the furniture that you are setting upon it.

2. If you're not in the market for a larger rug and want to work with what you have, just make sure that all of your furniture is touching the rug proportionately.

3. A great and budget-friendly way to cover the floor of a larger room is to layer. Use an inexpensive, neutral jute rug as the base and place smaller, more interesting rugs or cow hides on top of it. This way you can benefit from the look of the smaller pieces without them feeling awkward in a space that's too large for them.

4. Paint a floor with a bold color wash. (For the best results, have your floors painted by professionals.) Use half acrylic paint and half water, finishing with a thick coat of polyurethane on top. This will allow the grain of the wood to stay visible through the color.

5. Be imaginative with tiles. Avoid expensive, specialty tiles by creating your own. Cut down larger-size inexpensive tiles and repurpose them. In our bathroom, we broke up an affordable marble tile into 12 x 4 inch pieces to create a herringbone pattern.

A grid of open shelves with a strict color scheme—white, clear, silver—feels cohesive. Candylike hourglasses inject colors and curves.

6

SHELVES +
VIGNETTES

SHELVES +
VIGNETTES
WE LOVE

smart ideas for every
room in the house

living room

Sculptural wood shelves double as
wall art and elevate collections of
bowls, vintage vases, and books. A
floor-hugging shelf spanning the
length of the room lowers the eye
and speaks to loungey seating for a
cozy, stay-awhile vibe.

entryway

An industrial shelf packed with well-loved film boxes proves everyday objects can be stylishly stored in plain sight. The volume of items is what saves the scheme; just one or two boxes might look random. A red silk lamp picks up on the colors and adds just the right finishing touch.

office

Skeletal shelves blend in rather than scream for attention, allowing wallpaper and art to dominate. A symmetrical setup is smart in an office—it instills order and a sense of professionalism.

hallway

A slim arched alcove feels substantial thanks to accessories that play to its strengths: Stacks of books add height, and art is hung right to the top to extend your gaze as much as possible. A stool below can be easily grabbed when needed.

bathroom

When guests arrive, use vignettes to draw attention away from problem areas. Here, stacks of vintage records and an old-school phonograph block an ugly window and feel dreamy against Fornasetti cloud-print wallpaper.

HANDBOOK

shelf styles

	why we love it	*take note*
floating	Shelves that appear to levitate thanks to hidden brackets are clean and streamlined. They take up minimal space and can be mounted over furniture and in awkward spaces, like the wall under the stairs.	Not the easiest to install, so enlist the help of a friend or professional.
built-in	Making the most of otherwise vacant wall space, built-ins work well lining the wall of a living room or library. We've also seen them elegantly flanking a fireplace, or as a complement to kitchen cabinets.	It will be very hard work to move or eliminate a built-in, so think about location carefully.
fixed-bracket	Brackets attach to the wall, allowing you to place shelves at any height—from the floor up to the ceiling—and move them around with ease.	Go for white brackets or paint them the same color as the wall so they fade away. Metal brackets lend an industrial feel.
freestanding	Stand-alone systems can move from the bedroom to the living room to the kids' room whenever your storage needs change.	Freestanding shelves can delineate space within a room—two-sided versions double the functionality.
corner *(opposite page)*	Always charming, these space-saving options utilize wall junctions and are perfect for displaying a collection.	Opt for modern, clean-cut versions or paint a traditional piece a fresh, vibrant color so the look isn't too sugary sweet.

STYLE
STATEMENTS

snapshots of inspiring ideas

rustic

the mood: earthy, tactile, warm.

styling notes: Thick floating shelves made of reclaimed wood ground a collection of vintage Heath ceramics. Introducing a few reflective elements offers a breather from the matte pieces.

collected

the mood: layered, well-traveled, fun.

styling notes: At first glance, it may seem there's no rhyme or reason to this array, but key decorating principles are at play. The stripes on the shade mirror the striated sideboard and feel nautical, as does the collection of objects: a mermaid, a sailboat, a fish. The pair of lamps bookend the vignette, giving it structure.

classic

the mood: striking, refined, elegant.

styling notes: Dark and light paint create a chiaroscuro effect, with white accessories nestled within a fireplace opening that's painted dusky brown. Sculptural objects loosen up the gridded art display; the candlestick adds height, and, by breaking the line of the frame, acts as a visual connector.

coastal

the mood: energizing, thoughtful, happy.

styling notes: A beachy travel theme connects various elements, from driftwood candlesticks to whale bookends. Limiting the palette to the colors of the seaside—turquoise, brown, sand—ensures the scheme stays afloat.

get the look

---

serene

A curved niche filled with milky white ceramics feels as beautiful as a window view.
Stacks upon stacks—dishes on books—add subtle texture. Muted pastels allow shapes to demand
attention, from a scalloped platter to a hobnail bowl and curvy candlestick.

transparent sculpture

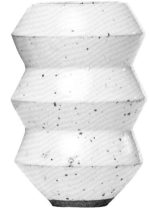

book as art

sculptural vase

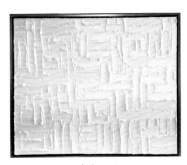

calming art

matte white round vase

beige bowl

glass bowl

Turn to page 270 for information on these products.

STYLE SCHOOL

stellar shelf styling

color for calm
Allow a few main colors to headline the show. Maybe jewel tones with touches of gold (shown opposite), neutrals, black and white, or shades of blue. Establishing a palette makes shelves feel pulled together. What colors should you choose? Look to the furnishings in your room.

horizontal + vertical lines
Stacks of books feel strangely serene; upright books feel poised and proper. Go for a mix of both. Horizontal books can serve as pedestals for accessories and bookends for open-sided shelves. Use sculptures to flank clusters of vertical books. Position titles at or near the shelf's edge.

depth and dimension
Lean some pieces of art, a mirror, or pretty books against the back wall to give the shelf depth and draw you in.

varied landscape
When placing objects, imagine looking at a cityscape, where there's a mix of heights rather than a strict lineup. Short, medium, and tall items keep the eye darting around.

points of light
Use museum-worthy artwork lights, a mini table lamp, or clip-on lights to give certain spots a sense of gravitas.

symmetry, shaken up
Most shelves can be loose and playful but instill some with a sense of order—two vases flanking a stack of books, or a sculpture in the center.

personal ephemera
It's about putting a piece of yourself on display. Lean a baby photo against a row of books, tuck a piece of pottery you made as a child under a glass cloche. Think of each shelf as its own story.

thoughtful contrast
Clustering objects can show off their individuality: a tall vase with a short, chunky pitcher, or a smooth concrete bowl atop a slab of rough-cut wood. Try rustic baskets on sleek industrial shelves, a mod sculpture on traditional shelves.

crowning achievement
The eye is always drawn up, so treat high shelves with intention. Here, trophy-like antlers preside over the festivities.

(btw)

As you style your shelves, take a step back and view them from across the room. Gauge overall balance: Are there too many small objects you can't see individually? Too many large items that make the shelf feel heavy? Play around.

styling shelving in a...

kitchen

Wood shelves are welcome in a kitchen, as they warm up a room dominated by functional fixtures. Break up the sea of ceramics and glass with a stack of wooden cutting boards or rustic utensils propped in a crock.

Vary tones, textures, and colors so your kitchen doesn't feel like a store display. (If things do start feeling "commercial," pepper in some non-kitchen items, like a piece of art behind a row of glasses.)

Keep the items you grab most— mugs, bowls, water glasses— within reach. Place less-used wares (ramekins, sake cups) up top.

Pile on the plates—you want shelves to feel loaded and bountiful and still look stocked even with items in the dishwasher.

If you're short on space, attach small hooks to the bottom of a shelf for teacups or mugs.

bathroom

The wall above the toilet is begging for shelves—this would be otherwise wasted space. Paint shelves the same color as the walls so they disappear.

In a small room (especially one with no medicine cabinet), all surfaces have to work hard. The top of the toilet can serve as a shelf for holding small items. Stash extra towels on a shelf under the sink.

Tight spaces need consistency, so use the same material for baskets (in this case, seagrass), and introduce a few other materials as well, like glass or even an unused ceramic sugar bowl, so the look isn't too staged.

Use the baskets for freeing up cabinet space and containing particularly unruly items like hairdryers, curling irons, and brushes.

White accents calm the mind: Think rolled white towels, white candles, a hydrangea tucked into a bottle.

Antique furnishings (like the mirror here) make the bathroom feel like an escape (bed and breakfast, anyone?).

Wood takes the starkness out of a room dominated by hard surfaces. Different tones of wood can coexist, particularly when they share a weathered finish.

office

Built-in shelves tucked into an alcove make the most of usable space. The wash of white fosters a clean backdrop that does not distract.

Uniform storage on each shelf offers a tidy look. Have fun with it—labeling boxes with numbers turns looking for supplies into a scavenger hunt (in a good way). Filling glass jars with bright yellow pencils and old-school pink erasers turns useful items into decor.

Keep some baskets empty, waiting to be filled. Too much stuff will clutter up your mind—a bit of space here and there allows inspiration to strike.

A fresh bloom invigorates a space where natural light is at a minimum.

Wall hooks keep totes and backpacks off the floor.

kids' room

Instill good design sense from a young age. Forgo laminate shelves for gorgeous wood that you'll appreciate, too.

See-through storage for color-sorted toys adds polish and order where you'd typically find chaos.

Organize shelves by type—books on one level, toys on another, mementos grouped together.

One offbeat object can distract from a sea of uniformity. Here, a wooden robot lightens the mood.

Pocket-size plants let kids take pride in growing their own greenery.

inspiring style:

lili diallo

(on minimalism)

Lili Diallo, style consultant and interior brand designer for fashion industry giants, is also the founder of jelovestudio.com, and the online magazine Billie.

Once an avid collector of objects, Lili explains her "less is more" evolution: "Now I am more about the experience. I would rather focus on having only special things, and fewer of them, in my home."

Long gone are the days when Lili was a collector. "Part of my job as a stylist was to find objects. I had an affinity for finding beautiful things, vintage French linens, glass objects, etc., but I became overwhelmed by their uselessness."

These days, for things to have a place in Lili's home, they must serve a purpose. Form and function are most important. A good example is her prized possession, a 1940s Jacques Adnet lamp. Yes, of course it's beautiful, but it also has a use.

Lili still has one weakness as a collector: jewelry. She loves stones and gold and silver. She is particularly drawn to the artistry of Native American jewelry, especially handcrafted, one-of-a-kind Navajo pieces.

lili's tips

1. Every item in your house should ideally be able to stand alone in its brilliance. Clear away things that can only come alive in a group. When there is less, each item becomes more heroic, and its beauty multiplies.

2. Instead of, say, eight objects on a bookshelf, pick just three. Make sure the items are connected and share a common thread, which can be the color or maybe the time period of the piece.

3. Make every effort to edit down all of your belongings. Just keep things that you love and the things you use. Less is more.

4. It is easy to convince people of the beauty of an object. But that very much depends on how you place it in the room. An object becomes a stronger statement when alone, or with a single companion piece.

dressing up the back

paint the back *and* shelves for a shadow-box feel. Or paint the back of each shelf a slightly different shade for an ombré effect.

wallpaper with a pretty floral, a punchy geometric, or with bold stripes.

fabric is a nice alternative to wallpaper.

beadboard feels charming and sweet. Keep it white or paint it deep gray.

wood shims (found at hardware stores) add gorgeous texture.

(btw)

If you're putting a bookcase against a wallpapered wall, pop off the back if you can—why cover up a pattern?

shop your home for 10 shelf + vignette staples

1. books

Books are representations of our passions, our histories, and give others glimpses into our interests. That being said, some books are better for display than others: Relegate your self-help guides to a private spot. Peek under a book jacket and you just might find a gem underneath—something textured and rustic and altogether better than that shiny paper cover.

2. sculptural objects
Large vases, pitchers, and bowls fill up space and have presence from afar. Fill with small stuff to give it visual oomph: Fill a glass ice bucket with wine corks, a bowl with vintage photos, or a jar with river rocks.

3. art
Pieces can be framed, unframed, a child's creation, or something found. Whatever it is, it should be loved.

4. clear items
Acrylic boxes and glass bowls are great for layering without blocking what's behind them.

5. the good stuff
Why relegate all that pretty cut crystal, porcelain, and family silver to the back of the cabinet? Take it out so you can truly appreciate it—you'll be amazed how sleek these pieces look next to modern items.

6. vacation mementos
A stunning postcard or piece of driftwood from the shore will make you happy every time you see it.

7. trays
A must for uniting random objects.

8. collections
Don't think you have one? Three like items make a collection, so look around and see what you find. Think mercury glass, salt and pepper shakers, or figurines.

9. reflective elements
Seek out items that catch light, like a mirrored box, a gilded frame, or a silver bowl.

10. fresh greens
Nothing brings an arrangement more to life than...life. Air plants and succulents are hardy choices that require minimal care.

4 prime places
for a vignette

1. bar cart

Edit down your bottles to the spirits you'll most likely serve—and to the prettiest; pour anything with questionable packaging into decanters—they make everything feel special. Always include something unexpected: a cactus, sculpture, stacks of cool books. The best trick for making a bar cart feel stylish: treating the wall behind it. Black paint gives the cart pictured here a moody quality. A leaned piece of art ties to the image on the wall, so the cart feels like an intentional part of the decor.

2. mantel

Balance the heft of a fireplace with a large piece of art, then use that colorway to dictate the rest of the scheme. Here, black and white reign, but a bright yellow vase filled with confectionary pink flowers lightens the mood and ties to the stack of colorful books. Aim for a mix of heights to keep the eye moving; a stack of books is a nice element to balance. Two leaning mirrors loosen up the scheme, while reflecting the ceiling to foster the illusion of height. Filling a nonworking or out-of-season fireplace with a plant gives the space life.

3. dresser

Think layers here. Echo the shape of the dresser with art and work forward, leaning a smaller piece in front and adding elements of various sizes, shapes, and colors. In a bedroom, a subdued color palette is soothing, and personal touches, like a pretty dish for favorite jewelry or a painting done by a friend, make sense. A mix of textures (shiny, matte, rough, smooth) and heights (high, low) creates an intriguing landscape.

(btw)

When you're happy with your vignette, take a photo of it. This way if you move stuff around for dusting (or a curious kid plays around with your perfect positioning), you can easily recreate the look.

4. coffee table

The best view is from above, so style accordingly. For a geometric take, choose items that mimic the shape of the table—boxes, books, and matchboxes fill up a square table and take on the effect of a gallery wall. Stacks are good—they give depth to a large horizontal plane. Include a plant or flowers for color. And don't forget a beautiful box to hide not-so-beautiful remote controls.

style skills:
use shelves to...

camouflage a platform bed

boost bathroom storage

modernize a media center

In a small space, tucking the bed into surrounding bookshelves makes sleeping quarters part of the story, and gives the space a dollhouse quality. Picture ledges display nighttime reading—and take the place of nightstands.

A powder room without a medicine cabinet gets a storage bump thanks to wall-mounted open shelving and a mirror with a frame deep enough to hold essentials like hand soap.

Metal shelving adds structure without the heft. Instead of piling up your cable box and modem, place them on separate shelves to break up the monotony and use strategically placed vases in front of cords. The controlled clutter of books and ephemera takes the focus off the TV—the striking, unexpected wallpaper doesn't hurt, either.

turn plants into wall art

sneak in a desk

serve up martinis

A mini perch for plants elevates greenery to art status. Set pots at different heights for a cute vertical garden.

Space-saving heaven: Midcentury shelves moonlight as office space without cutting into square footage. Since the wood matches other elements, the setup can stay in the living room without stressing you out.

The convenience of a built-in shelf makes a spirited spot for nightcap necessities.

inspiring style:

claire zinnecker
(on shelves + vignettes)

Austin, Texas–based designer Claire Zinnecker describes her pared-down style as "slightly Scandinavian with a splash of Japanese minimalism." She goes for simple, clean lines and white walls, but then layers with color, personality, and quirky details. Working with a blank slate means that the "fun stuff" becomes more noticeable. "I paint my walls white so I can paint my door pink, and it works."

She's also a big DIY-er. "Our homes are our sanctuaries and they should be exactly what we want them to be. That's what's so fun about design and even more fun about DIY design. If I need something, I think of the solution and then I create it, instead of going online and buying it."

"Design for the way you live," Claire suggests. There is no one recipe to follow.

claire's tips

1. Think of your vignette as a page to read: You want the eye to travel along it easily, so shoot for balance.

2. An easy recipe for a shelf: Stack three to five books upright and then three to five sideways with a knickknack or small plant on top. Place a piece of art or a few larger found objects next to the stacks.

3. Don't be afraid to be bold! Use bright colors or metallics to brighten any vignette, or an entire room.

4. Edit, edit, edit! Place everything, then step back and eliminate at least two pieces. Too much clutter can ruin your look.

5. Mix one-dimensional with two-dimensional, especially on a gallery wall. Incorporate things that otherwise might sit in a closet, like a camera or a hat. Change up your objects to keep your gallery current.

6. Plants add an organic element. Take advantage of the varying colors, shapes, and sizes they come in, and use them as the perfect space fillers.

A glass fixture mimics the shape of the table without hindering the view.

7

LIGHTING

LIGHTING
WE LOVE

smart ideas for every
room in the house

bathroom

Brass sconces with attenuated
arms make a statement and can
be angled when needed. Pairing
them with an antique side
table makes the bathroom
feel cohesive.

living room

A streamlined starburst makes a point in an otherwise quiet room. Bookshelf fixtures spotlight a collection of tomes and objects, while imparting an ambient glow.

dining room

A geometric fixture with an exposed bulb helps a charming dining nook feel modern. The open, delicate design allows it to be a focal point without weighing down the room.

kitchen

A lineup of milk-glass orbs breaks up a view of cabinetry and speaks to curvy-topped stools.

HANDBOOK

figuring out fixtures

table lamps
These are the cozy guys of the lighting world—they add character and intimacy, and provide subtle, diffused light to fill in shadows and flatter spaces and faces.

floor lamps
Perfect for illuminating the dark corners of a room, floor lamps work to provide directional and ambient illumination. For a pleasing layered effect, include torchères that shed light upward for ambience and others that shed light down for reading. To bring interest to the lower level of a room, consider a literal version of the term *floor lamp* with a sculptural glowing orb that sits right on the ground.

sconces
Space-saving sconces are multi-functional. You can use a single sconce over a desk, in a nook, or to highlight a piece of art (shown opposite), but in general they look best in pairs—flanking a fireplace, dining room buffet, entryway console, or a bed.

recessed lights
Also called high hats or can lights, these fixtures are embedded in the ceiling to stay out of the way (great for low ceilings). Stick to a small size—about 3 inches in diameter—for the most stylish look.

flush mounts
These hug the ceiling to provide bright, all-over light.

semi-flush mounts
Hanging about a foot down, they typically have more flair than flush mounts but are still high enough to provide head clearance.

pendants
Chandeliers and other fixtures that hang down can light a room (say, an entryway) or spotlight a task (above a kitchen island). Experiment with pendants in place of table lamps; imagine them alongside a sofa or bed.

beautiful bulbs that are just too pretty to hide

edison
The visible filament recalls Thomas Edison's original design. These are low-wattage, so are more for aesthetic appeal than illumination.

silver bowl
Dipped in a metallic finish that softens the light, they're also available with a gold tip.

cut crystal
A gorgeous surprise in a contemporary fixture.

round candelabra
Swap flame bulbs for these and your chandelier will feel instantly more inspired.

STYLE
STATEMENTS

snapshots of inspiring ideas

whimsical

the mood: bright, quaint, nostalgic.

styling notes: Swathed in black, a charming little chandelier gives edge to a room steering toward vintage.

eclectic

the mood: fierce, fearless, handsome.

styling notes: When paired with extreme elements like a glossy black four-poster bed, a cobalt overdyed rug, and graphic wallpaper, a rope chandelier feels less nautical than medieval, giving the room a unique voice.

minimalist

the mood: straightforward, calm, beautifully bare.

styling notes: A couldn't-be-simpler wall-mounted fixture makes nightstands unnecessary and folds flat when not in use. The pared down furnishings help strip away stress—just what you want in a bedroom.

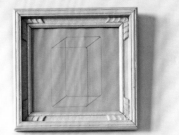

industrial

White metal pendants bring utilitarian appeal and much-needed curves to a kitchen's horizontal lines, from the tiled island and backsplash to the rectangular glass table. Wood-paneled walls and mismatched chairs balance the cool of the fixtures and accessories: a pot-scrubber faucet, a stainless-steel counter, and a metal bar for dish towels and utensils.

STYLE SCHOOL

what every room needs

The secret to a well-lit room? Not being able to immediately tell how it's lit. When you walk into a space with perfectly diffused light, it just feels right and comfortable, like you could hang out there all day.

You'll want a mix of:

ambient light: General illumination that covers the whole room.

task light: Bright light for performing jobs (chopping veggies, applying mascara, working at home).

accent light: Spotlights on specific areas, from a cool plant to a bookcase.

a happy medium:
A too-bright room will feel institutional and off-putting; a too-dim room, particularly during the day, will feel dingy. Use lights of different brightness to draw attention to various areas.

different sources:
Overheads mimic the sun in that they brighten large swaths of space—but on their own they create shadows and will tire you out. Supplement with other fixtures to evenly distribute light or your home will feel like a convention center. A mix of sources delivers evenly distributed light and a soothing, flattering glow. Think soft pools of light rather than a beam from just one source.

dimmers galore:
In addition to saving energy, dimmers offer the flexibility to switch from bright light to soft chill-out light at a moment's notice. Installing a dimmer is an easy job for an electrician. Even easier? Buying a clip-on dimmer that attaches to your lamp cord.

natural light:
If one room gets spectacular sun and an adjacent one much less, consider replacing standard interior doors with glass-paned versions to filter light through multiple spots.

separate control:
Put sources on different switches: The worst is flicking one switch and lighting up the entire room like a stage set.

room-by-room lighting guide

living room

A mix of lighting is not only visually appealing, it's functional. Forgo harsh overheads if you can for softer table and floor lamps. Use small lamps to illuminate unexpected spots, like a mantel. Give as many chairs as you can a reading light. Use three-way bulbs to accommodate different moods. And vary the shades rather than repeating one type throughout the room—a drum shade, hexagon, and empire can peacefully coexist and make a space feel collected and intriguing. That being said, you don't want too many shades, or you run the risk of your room looking like a showroom.

dining room

Err on the large side—if a fixture is too small for the space, it will feel like an afterthought rather than a showstopper, which is what this room craves. Go for something that feels like an anomaly—a statement piece with rebel tendencies. Hang the fixture so the bottom is 30 to 34 inches above the table; the width of the fixture should be one-third the length of the table. High ceilings can handle long cylinders or drippy cascading designs; low ceilings prefer a fixture that spreads more horizontally. Supplement with sconces or a small lamp on a buffet for extra warmth—and don't forget candlelight.

hallway

Hang pendants low enough so that you can appreciate their beauty, but high enough that they won't feel in the way: Roughly 7 feet from the floor is the sweet spot. Topping a console with a lamp (or sconces, if you're tight on space, hung about 6 feet from the floor) is a welcoming touch. In a hallway, you'll ideally want light every 8 to 10 feet; if you have a long hallway, supplement with sconces.

bedroom

Position reading lamps or swing-arm sconces so that they shed light on the bed without pointing directly at it. To prevent shadows when reading, you'll want the bottom of the shade to be between your head and the book when you're sitting up in bed—typically this comes to 20 inches above the mattress. Choose a light-colored shade—black looks cool but may not throw enough light for reading. If you don't want to be bound by symmetrical table lamps, you can use two different styles as long as they're of similar heights (stack some books under the shorter one if necessary) and have the same material shade so they shed uniform light.

bathroom

The worst possible light for your bathroom? One overhead fixture, which will throw too much light on your forehead—creating shadows under your eyes, nose, and chin. The ideal situation: a 75-watt overhead with two 60-watt lights flanking the mirror at eye level (about 36 to 40 inches apart), providing an even cross-light (with little glare) that sweeps across your face.

kids' room

Table and floor lamps have toppling potential. Use pretty pendants instead, strategically placed near the bed for reading. Clip-on fixtures are affordable and sweet.

kitchen

You'll want overheads for all-over ambience, plus focused light where you cook. Pendants are best 28 to 34 inches above an island, starting 12 to 15 inches in from either end. Think carefully about materials; rich pendants can make moderately priced kitchens look custom. Consider fitting glass-door cabinets with interior lights for nighttime glimmer.

style skills:
use lighting to...

transition between two spaces

create a magical glow

Prominent light fixtures can visually connect adjacent rooms, bringing a sense of balance and order by giving the eye something to focus on. The styles don't have to be the same, but scale and colors should be consistent for maximum impact.

Hanging multiple George Nelson lamps at various heights takes on the effect of hot-air balloons, lending drama to a large space. At nighttime, it's like a starry sky.

inject humor

trick out a tub

In a room that feels somewhat serious (here, an extra-tall screen/headboard is cool but a bit imposing), bringing in a lighthearted lamp could be just the icebreaker a space needs.

An elaborate fixture in the bathroom is pure decadence. For safety, hang it at least eight feet above the tub.

inspiring style:

workstead
(on easy lighting solutions)

Swiss-born Stefanie Brechbuehler and her Southern partner, Robert Highsmith, are interior designers and the co-creators of the lighting company Workstead. Necessity led them to design their first lighting fixture—created for an older brownstone in Brooklyn. Robert explains, "There was a lot of woodwork, and all the electrical boxes were in strange places. The dining table needed to be in the middle of the room, but the junction box was weirdly off-center." So the couple created a unique chandelier as a way to cope with the limitations of the room—it had the utility of an industrial light fixture but the flexibility of a sculpture in that it could be easily moved. The pair, who have long admired French lighting designers as well as historic American lighting manufacturers, have mixed their tastes to design exquisite yet simple lighting solutions.

workstead's tips

1. Always, always have all your light switches on a dimmer, no matter what.

2. A great floor lamp is a perfect solution for a dark corner. If you find a good one, it will bring a quality of warmth and coziness to the room.

3. Avoid clear bulbs. Instead, use soft, frosted bulbs for shaded fixtures as well as pendants, which give off a much prettier light.

4. A cheap and cheerful way to replace canned, recessed lighting is to use little porcelain sockets with oversize, 6-inch, frosted bulbs. (And don't forget to have them on a dimmer!)

5. Rooms should be lit in layers. A person should never walk into a room, flip a switch, and have five lights blasting down from cans. Instead, start with overall ambient ceiling light and then add an accent pendant or a chandelier. Try a floor lamp in the corner, a tiny lamp on a bookshelf, and perhaps an artistic glowing light in a corner. This combination will create an interesting mood in the room.

6. If you're renting, don't forget about plug-in sconces. They're easily installed at eye level and they bring so much to a room.

A tiger print sheet and pillowcase and a few friendly faces temper the lines of wood-paneled walls and a geometric daybed.

8

SOFT STUFF

SOFT
STUFF
WE LOVE

smart ideas for every
room in the house

bedroom

A sheepskin rug rounds
out an angular, minimalist
platform bed and serves as
a source of plush texture.

bathroom

Hung on delicate brass hooks, tasseled towels add texture, color, and pattern to an all-white bath.

living room

Hiding gorgeous super-wide-plank floors under a rug would be a shame. Instead, throw pillows work hard to compensate by pulling colors from the botanical art. Gauzy white curtains framing the doors to the garden create an airy entry.

HANDBOOK
throw pillows

shape

square pillows provide the best all-over back support.

rectangular pillows and **cylindrical** bolsters are perfectly suited for a sofa's midpoint. Bolsters work well with leather sofas as they don't slip down the way other shapes do.

circular pillows are sweet, soften the straight lines of seating, and offer an unexpected change of pace.

size

Eighteen-inch pillows look right on most sofas, but try 16-inch options on seating with low backs and 20- or 24-inch versions on large, overstuffed sofas and chairs. When in doubt, err on the large size. In general, it's best to go for a few large pillows rather than a jumble of smaller ones, which have the tendency to look messy.

fill

A foam and polyester combination keeps its shape, but may feel stiff. Down and feathers are lightweight and lush, though they'll need fluffing on occasion. Consider removable covers that can be washed and swapped out easily.

bottom layer: sheets

cotton

The best? Egyptian cotton—it's extremely supple and durable. Don't worry so much about thread count (the type of cotton is more important). Next in line, and less expensive, is pima cotton. You'll find two weaves: percale (matte, crisp, and cool—nice if you get overheated at night) and sateen (thick, lustrous, smooth, and warm). Feel sheets before buying to sense if they're warm or cool to the touch—that's a matter of personal preference.

linen

An all-weather, versatile choice: thick for winter, cool for summer. And the more you wash it, the better it gets.

silk

Elegant and sensuous, silk makes crawling into bed extra exciting. And no, good quality silk sheets don't require dry-cleaning; just wash on gentle using cold water and silk-friendly detergent. Silk may lose some luster over time, but it'll get softer.

middle layer: duvets and covers

down

The soft, fluffy filling is warm and lightweight—a great combination. When shopping around, compare fill power, which is the amount of down per ounce. A fill power of 600 is great, but 500 might be preferable if you get warm at night. Goose and duck down are similar, but goose down's large, lofty clusters make it slightly better at insulating.

down alternative

Man-made fillings, such as rayon or polyester are cheaper, easier to maintain, and ideal for allergy-sufferers. But the stuffing tends to feel heavy, and it's not as adept at regulating temperature.

duvet covers

Cotton is the most common choice. Look for a thread count of at least 300 tpi to ensure down feathers won't poke through.

top layer: throws

These are finishing touches for extra warmth that you can switch out seasonally or whenever you need a change. Place a throw at the foot of the bed folded in thirds, so it can easily straighten when you need to pull it up. Trim or fringe adds another layer of detail.

(btw)

Steer clear of synthetic sheets like polyester, acrylic, and nylon. Though their low price point and wrinkle-resistance may be tempting, a bed just isn't the place to go faux. Synthetic sheets don't feel as soft as other materials, are prone to pilling, and can absorb oil, making stains tough to remove.

10 tactile treats for every home

1. luxurious white sheets make other bedroom adornment unnecessary (shown this page).

2. embroidered tablecloths give everyday affairs a handcrafted appeal.

3. tasseled welcome mats are flirty and functional.

4. turkish hand towels offer a refreshing twist from terrycloth.

5. mohair throws are lightweight but really warm—the ideal combination for movie nights.

6. fluffy white towels bring to mind hotel serenity.

7. a sheepskin can transform a cold hard bench into a shaggy-chic delight (shown opposite, top left).

8. moroccan floor cushions signal guests to take a load off (shown opposite, top right).

9. a flatweave rug in the bathroom is decadent but also smart—it's made to withstand traffic (shown opposite, bottom left).

10. layered coverlets turn a bed into a textural haven (shown opposite, bottom right).

STYLE STATEMENTS

snapshots of inspiring ideas

traditional

the mood: refined, rich, vintage.

styling notes: A painterly textile turns a formal headboard into abstract art and acts as a bridge between bright white linens and a rich maroon wall. Subtle details, like nailhead, pom-pom trim, and a preppy striped bed skirt feel like a treat when you realize they're there. A nubby blanket and a pair of velvet ottomans anchor the scene.

graphic

the mood: abstract, fresh, spare.

styling notes: A Marimekko tapestry (secured to the ceiling with ropes threaded through grommets) distracts from tight quarters and recalls a high-seas adventure. The swirly pattern and scalloped pillows soften the boxy space. The black bed skirt makes the bed feel like it's floating, another small-space trick.

modern

the mood: clean, colorful, modern.

styling notes: A tufted headboard gets a hit of pattern and color thanks to a family of throw pillows in lush materials. Even the black-and-white art adds a layer of softness in its own sophisticated way.

get the look

cottage

Matching sheets to wallpaper makes the room feel "done." The headboard's wings carve out a cozy enclosure, and the ample padded back makes reading in bed easy. The bed is casually made—no frills, starch, or strict tuck-action here—so it feels inviting and realistic.

striped throw pillow

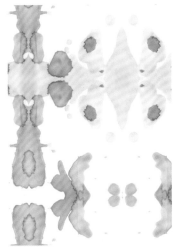

pastel wallpaper

cotton herringbone throw

Pondicherry headboard

linen throwbed

colonial side table

sky blue bedding

Turn to page 270 for information on these products.

STYLE
SCHOOL

alternative
headboards

fabric

Patterned curtains that complement the bedspread create a sleeping nook that feels regal.

flag

This vintage flag flies high—extending past the bed frame and up to the ceiling to make the room feel taller. Placing the flag behind an industrial bed frame makes it feel less dorm room, more design-forward. And the elegant hanging method—nails hammered directly through—is easy and unexpected.

mirror

A tall mirrored headboard makes a room feel brighter, bigger, taller, and more glamorous. To offset the glass, a sheer canopy is hung from the ceiling.

screen

Tucked behind an upholstered headboard, a screen provides another layer, widening the room and harmonizing with wooden beams, rattan shades, and a hanging wicker chair.

style skills:
use soft stuff to...

warm up a cold bathroom

make a corner cushy

Colorful Turkish rugs take the chill out of a tiled floor, while blasting white surfaces with mesmerizing color and pattern. Ruffly top-down, bottom-up shades offer privacy and let in light from above. "Real" curtains frame the large window, making the space feel like a true retreat.

Layering a thick sheepskin over a thin cowhide turns a sunny section of nursery into a story-time spot. The giant teddy bear softens the corner and acts as a backrest. Sheer curtains gently break at the floor and filter light.

mellow the lines of hard furnishings

create a bed you never want to leave

Sheepskin rugs make everything they land on infinitely cozier (these low-cost versions from Ikea take two side chairs from proper to plush). Toss one on a wooden bench, a rattan chaise, or the back of a wire Bertoia chair. They're even great for softening something already soft; try one in the corner of a sectional to break up the large expanse and watch guests—and dogs and cats and kids—flock to it.

Sheets aren't the place to skimp. Here, layers of sumptuous Matteo bed linens feel like heaven and pool at the floor. Mixing shades of creamy white offers subtle dimension; casually tossed pillows signal laid-back luxury. Backed against a window with billowy white curtains, the bed takes on an ethereal quality.

window treatments

youthful energy

Mixed prints from floor to ceiling give a nursery global glamour rather than childlike charm.

tactile flourish

A macrame curtain is a chic choice for filtering light and looks particularly striking next to a sculptural plant.

graceful + groovy

The subtle beaded print of a linen shade is like a modern version of a '70s classic.

considerations

curtains

length: A good standard is to allow curtains to kiss the floor (half an inch above is fine, as well). Too short and they'll look geeky; too long and they'll collect dust. There are exceptions, though—a casual, informal space might be able to pull off curtains a bit shorter; a formal room could benefit from a romantic pooling on the floor.

width: Buy enough fabric—you'll need fullness for the drape to look right. Figure you'll need 1.5 to twice the width of the window. Hang rods 6 to 8 inches beyond the frame on each side, or wider to make windows appear bigger.

linings: Unless you want curtains to diffuse light or blow in the breeze, it's usually a good idea to get the fabric lined. Linings protect from sun damage, dirt, and condensation. They also add insulation. Decoratively, linings hide seams and stitch holes, keep patterns prominent, and help fabric drape with confidence. Consider blackout liners for bedrooms or nurseries.

shades

inside mounts: The cleanest, most tailored—and most common—application that allows window moldings to be seen and appreciated. They can make a small window look even smaller, though. When measuring, round down to the nearest $\frac{1}{8}$ inch so shades have enough space to glide up and down without snagging the frame.

outside mounts: Best for privacy and light control, and for masking less-than-desirable window frames. The rod can be mounted on the window molding or outside of it; the latter makes the window appear bigger.

inspiring style:

frances merrill
(on mixing textiles)

Interior designer Frances Merrill's love of textiles started when she was young. "I remember teaching myself to sew as a child and coming to the realization that the only really interesting part of what I had made was the actual design of the material." She went on to intern for the world-renowned Jim Thompson Thai Silk Company in Bangkok and later studied textile design in Los Angeles.

"I love when things are put together in a new way," says Frances. "By mixing genres of textiles you can personalize a room." Curtains, throw cushions, shams, and upholstery are all great ways to add that second, lived-in layer to a room. "I especially love vintage fabrics because of the muted and faded colors. It's also wonderful to add something that is handmade to the mix."

"As a designer, my favorite textile is a tiny scrap of a Japanese Boro, which is all that is left of a larger piece I once wrapped around my couch cushions. Everyone in my office laughs at me because, without fail, this tiny piece makes it into every client presentation—even when I have a huge box of fabrics I love! I use the Boro to represent all the antique textiles that we will buy for the client."

frances's tips

1. To add some depth to your bedroom, hang an interesting piece of fabric in place of a headboard, or drape some material over an existing headboard.

2. There are no rules for throw pillows, but keep this in mind when layering them: Try something vintage, something soft, something striped; and, of course, something jewel-toned. Experiment! Play with color, pattern, and texture.

3. To make the most of a cheap pillow find from Etsy or eBay, replace the pillow back with velvet or add a shiny satin welt (a covered cord sewn into a seam as trim) for character. A fun striped material works well for the piping.

4. Quilts are another way to add texture and color to a room. They are especially great for a kids' room and can be a way to bring in a vintage element.

5. For drapes, try an inexpensive linen in a solid color—ideally a pretty jewel-tone. Use as much yardage as possible, covering the entire wall. This way, open or closed, the drapes will transform the room. Consider lining the drapes in the same solid color so the room looks really bright and vibrant from the street outside.

Sculptural plants and round accents smooth out the edges of a bathroom heavy on hard surfaces (brick, tile, cement, glass, wood).

9

PLANTS +
FLOWERS

PLANTS
+ FLOWERS
WE LOVE

smart ideas for every
room in the house

dining room

A lineup of ferns in mismatched
ceramic pots feels right at home
on a rustic table and lightens up
a raw brick wall.

kitchen

Charming topiaries flanking the sink lend soothing symmetry and direct the eye to the textured wood ceiling.

outside

Herbs aplenty: A lush garden of rosemary, laurel, coriander, and parsley surrounds a sundial.

office

A vertical succulent garden creates a stunning backdrop for a vibrant seating area, where a French settee upholstered with Japanese shibori cloth is paired with an African Bamileke table.

HANDBOOK

haute houseplants

	boston fern	string of pearls	split-leaf philodendron
why we love it	Oversize and fantastically frilly, it's a textural treat.	With its fleshy, pealike foliage, this aptly named succulent is botanical jewelry for your home.	Its tropical, large-scale leaves are room-defining—even just one leaf peeking out of a vase will look like art.
take note	Indirect light and high humidity will keep it happy, so hang near a window and switch on a humidifier if you have one. Its heavy, leathery leaves sometimes block moisture intake—so water near the base.	Place in bright light and water every week; in winter you can get away with once a month. Trim any stems that have lost their "pearls" to keep it looking full.	This species prefers to be out of the sun and dry, so only water once a week.
ideal vessel	The plant's ancient roots (figuratively speaking) make it an ideal candidate for a contrasting modern planter. A fun, ceramic urn elevates the whimsical nature of the plant and gives it a bit of polish.	Let it cascade over a sleek, white hanging planter, a crisp backdrop that lets the detailed shape of the plant truly shine.	A simple black cylindrical planter perfectly complements the big modern leaves; place against a white wall so the graphic nature can truly be appreciated.

	snake plant	staghorn fern	succulents
why we love it	Super-straight, sword-shaped leaves add architectural edge—great for filling a corner or adding height to a dresser or sideboard.	Artistic and free-spirited, this wall-mountable air plant doubles as sculpture.	Irresistibly adorable mini sculptures range from spiked and fuzzy to plump and round.
take note	You can neglect it and it'll still be your friend; it lives on minimal light and water. Just don't overwater—the roots can rot.	Mist daily and dunk the base in water weekly. Give it some light and use a humidifier if your space is dry.	Incredibly easy to care for; most like bright light and for soil to completely dry out between waterings.
ideal vessel	Go midcentury here—the sharp angles suit the leaves. It absorbs carbon dioxide and releases oxygen during the night (most plants do so during the day), so place in your bedroom for a breath of fresh air.	Mount onto wood or tuck inside a hanging glass orb to make the unusual species look museum-worthy. Place above a desk or dresser, or hang en masse for extra oomph.	Fill a simple pot with a variety of potted succulents in different shapes and hues. Place on a coffee table so you can take in views from above. Also great as a centerpiece, as their short stature won't block sight lines.

our favorite statement trees

	rubber tree	fiddle-leaf fig tree	kentia palm
why we love it	Its broad, oval leaves are super shiny and leather-like. Plus it's tough to kill and helps purify the air. (Fun fact: The name comes from the sticky sap emitted if injured.)	Designers can't get enough of the large, violin-shaped leaves, which punctuate a room with personality.	Graceful and arching, it can handle low light, underwatering, roughhousing, and general neglect. Totally low-maintenance.
take note	It thrives on indirect light; place next to gauzy curtains.	These trees stretch out and make themselves comfortable, so you might as well pick a roomy spot (indirect light, please) before things get hectic.	Place in a sunny spot, water regularly, and mist monthly to hydrate and remove any dust buildup. Kentia palms can grow up to 10 feet tall, so rooms with high ceilings are best.
ideal vessel	An oval-shaped planter mimics the shape of the leaves; choosing one that's matte will play off their glossiness.	Fiddle-leaf figs and oversize baskets are a perfect match. Their colors and textures are complementary (and photograph well together)!	A hefty, heavy planter (with drainage holes) is key, to avoid tipping and to balance out the delicate fronds. Play up its tropical nature with a fun color, like cobalt blue.

	dragon tree	lemon tree	banana tree
why we love it	Spiky, modern, and graphic, with branches you can angle and twist to your liking, it's an amazing accent for a clean-lined, contemporary space.	The next best thing to a holiday in Capri. It's always either flowering or growing lemons and can be moved outdoors in warm weather.	Exotic and tropical, with supersize floppy leaves, it's perfect for softening corners.
take note	Avoid direct sun—stick to moderate to bright light instead.	Consider a dwarf variety—it won't crowd your living space. Citrus trees need at least eight hours of light a day, so place in a south-facing window. Water regularly and mist in winter.	These need 12 hours of light a day, so place in a sunny spot. Mist regularly, and wipe down leaves now and then to remove dust. They can get big; if space is a concern, consider a dwarf variety.
ideal vessel	A sleek, white planter complements the geometry of the leaves.	An old-school terra-cotta pot will transport you to the old world. Get one with drainage holes, and place stones in the drainage dish for air circulation.	A square container contrasts the round leaves nicely, but go big—you'll need something sizable to handle the roots.

STYLE
STATEMENTS

snapshots of inspiring ideas

striking

the mood: lush, riotous, colorful.

styling notes: Thanks to a massive bouquet of lilacs, a handsome black-and-white scheme gets a shot of color without the commitment. Placing the arrangement on a low stool allows it to be appreciated from above.

bohemian

the mood: calm, airy, friendly.

styling notes: The shiny leaves of a fiddle leaf fig spruce up an empty corner and reflect natural light. Dotting the space with small plants—on the windowsill, the coffee table, up high, down low—gives the subdued room a sense of rhythm.

romantic

the mood: bright, playful, optimistic.

styling notes: Why not match flowers to art?
A pretty-in-pink print (*Peonies*, by Kate Schelter) melds
with gorgeous flowers that are actually made of crepe
paper, a beautiful notion by flower artist Livia Cetti.

architectural

the mood: spare, clean, modern.

styling notes: Treat plants like cut flowers by tucking
tropical fronds into vessels—it's an easy way to add color.

fresh

Topping a mantel with an array of fresh flowers in individual vases (some tall, some squat) is a great way to create an ever-changing array. Species that curve and trail break the stark lines of a marble fireplace; a palm tree adds edge. Clusters of flowers throughout the space give each seat a brush with nature.

style standoff

dark flowers vs. white flowers

dark flowers are unexpected and cool. Go for deep hues only—jet black, burgundy, deep brown—or add a few white moments (like heuchera or white lavender) for contrast. Here, purple-flowering oregano, offset by black scabiosa and an extra-tall stem of meadow rue, foster a scene of almost accidental beauty. Pairing a solid and a translucent vase in the same tone adds interest.

white flowers can feel poetic and pure in winter and fresh and fearless in summer. In a white vessel, greenery pops and blooms blend beautifully. We particularly love white roses, hydrangea (cottage charm at its best), and fragrant, dainty paperwhites.

style standoff

wide-neck vessels vs. narrow-neck vessels

wide necks let stems breathe, creating lush, loose displays that allow flower faces to be seen from all angles. If things are flopping all over the place, use floral foam to bring the arrangement back to normalcy. Works best with thick stems and large blooms (pepper in smaller buds to fill in gaps).

narrow necks are the ones to reach for if you're a novice at flower arranging—they corral flowers artfully and make you look like a pro. If there's room, tuck in a few leaves to offset the blooms.

STYLE SCHOOL

bouquet basics

1. start with greens.
Sturdy foliage acts as a structure to keep flowers in place. Think stiff but full and crisscross stems to create a webbing.

2. tuck in flowers.
Choose big "faces" for maximum impact, like peonies, roses, and dahlias. Cut stems to different heights, clustering a few and singling out others. Loosen up the arrangement so it doesn't look too perfect—allow certain blooms to fall forward or back naturally rather than forcing them into submission.

3. fill gaps.
Feathery elements like ferns work well. You can also look to your yard for "filler" flowers—even weeds like Queen Anne's Lace can be beautiful.

kennesha's tips

1. Look at your space, and decide (based on ceiling height, empty places, etc.) which areas need the most attention. You want to create a space that is visually pleasing, one that guides the eye across or into a room.

2. Mix it up. Use indoor plants that have varying colors such as the Chinese evergreen, fern varieties like the Boston fern, bird's nest, staghorn, or dainty maidenhair fern. Try a philodendron to brighten a room. Add some height with a baby palm. Be sure that the plants you choose complement your personal style and will be able to thrive in the environment you've chosen.

3. Think outside the box when placing plants. Plants aren't just for living spaces like the kitchen, family room, or den. Pour a little "plant love" into spaces sometimes forgotten, like powder rooms and offices.

4. The popular fiddle-leaf fig can be a finicky one. If the fiddle isn't your friend, try other varieties of indoor plants like the mass cane or an easier-to-grow genus of ficus. If you're in an area like California or Arizona, you may be successful with a potted olive. That's the stuff dreams are made of! Sometimes if you purchase from them, nursery people will even make house calls to help ensure that your "plant babies" live a long, healthy life in their new home.

5. Let plants help you to style dinners and intimate gatherings. While using plants on the tabletop is great, placement above the table as a chandelier or hanging installation can help to create an amazing atmosphere by adding visual impact. Try using succulents or air plants tucked in small vessels and hung from a metal or wooden structure above the table.

inspiring style:

kennesha buycks
(on plants with personality)

Writer, blogger, inspirational stylist, and creative director of Restoration House, Kennesha Buycks takes inspiration from her Southern roots and her present life in the Pacific Northwest, where she lives with her family. Nature in all its glory—sunsets, mountains, lush vegetation—fuels Kennesha's creativity. Greenery enhances her lifestyle. Kennesha explains: "Adding plants to a room is essential, no matter the color scheme or how large or small the space. Not only do indoor plants bring life and personality to a 'dead' space, certain varieties can also help make the air in your home a little cleaner."

style skills:
use plants +
flowers to...

set a hotel-worthy scene

invigorate a table

decorate a doorway

Adorning a nightstand with a couple of blooms makes bedtime brighter and mornings more doable.

Vibrant flowers clustered by type create a magical color-blocked tableau for a courtyard party.

In an entryway, suspending roses with simple ribbon provides a charming welcome for guests.

create living art

With antler-like fronds, staghorn ferns mounted and arranged into a grid make a poignant statement and feel at once precise and primitive.

sweeten a shelf

A charming cluster of flowers warms up a collection of cool (tending toward chilly) ceramics. Trailing tendrils hang down, uniting the shelves with a bohemian flow.

whip up a savory centerpiece

Transferred from their pots into mismatched teacups, herbs like sage, thyme, rue, and rosemary feel English garden–esque.

inspiring style:

new darlings
(on plants as accessories)

Robert and Christina Martinez, the husband-and-wife team behind the lifestyle blog New Darlings, use house plants as they would any other decorative accessory. "We're so inspired by the whole 1970s' house plant craze," they explain. "We have plants in every corner of our space."

new darlings' tips

1. For those who don't have a green thumb, start with very resilient cacti, air plants, and succulents. These plants are almost impossible to kill and require very little maintenance. Once-a-week watering and a light misting is sufficient. The less attention you give them, the more they thrive.

2. Experiment. Go beyond the typical pot you find at a plant nursery. Driftwood and glass terrariums work well for air plants, and are a perfect way to add a little greenery in the kitchen or on a coffee table. Mix and match ceramics, terra-cotta, glass, and baskets. Using baskets as containers for larger houseplants is a great way to go big without spending huge amounts of money.

3. Keep the taller fig and banana leaf plants in the corner near a window. Larger plants create depth and texture and bring a lot of life into a room.

4. Don't just place plants on a table; think out of the box. Elevation is good for fishhook or lipstick plants. Try setting them up on a mantel, so they cascade down, or place them on a plant swing. Have fun with groupings of pots in macramé hangers to add texture.

5. Factor in trial and error. Plants will tell you where they are the most happy. Move them around the house until they are in the perfect spot.

At a summer dinner party, streamlined place settings allow seasonal flowers in vintage brass vessels to deliver maximum impact.

10
ENTERTAINING

ENTERTAINING WE LOVE

smart ideas for every
room in the house

elegant lunch

Matching the centerpiece to the surroundings feels pulled-together and
polished. Feathery fronds speak to green-painted window and door frames,
while the hand-carved bowl picks up the tones of burnished copper chairs.

beach picnic

Seaside schemes should blend in to the environment rather than oppose it. Swap loud-patterned blankets for soft cotton sheets, and decant beverages with unsightly labels into glass bottles. Pack food that'll last: Rather than premade sandwiches that'll get soggy, bring a baguette with jams or other toppings that can be spread on-site.

rooftop drinks

Flower boxes and potted plants transform a city terrace into a bucolic escape. Large leaves moonlight as coasters and sprigs of green garnish drinks. A vintage box, repurposed into a pretty, portable bar, keeps cocktail necessities contained.

casual brunch

Break out the tablecloth for intimate affairs, and shake up serving pieces for interest. Rest butter in beautiful bowls; bring out a vintage coffee pot. An asymmetrical splay of luscious blooms is a surefire conversation-starter.

HANDBOOK

dining table
shapes
+ sizes

	why we love it	*take note*
round	Cozy and intimate, round tables allow everyone equal access to conversations. No sharp edges mean it's kid-friendly; also good for game night since the center is easy to reach.	If the table has a pedestal, apply pressure when shopping around to check sturdiness— wide pedestals are typically better.
rectangular *(opposite page)*	The most popular choice, this shape packs in lots of people, especially with a bench on one or both sides.	Guests can chat with those near them, but communicating with those at the opposite end of the table might require the whole party to engage in a group discussion.
square	Balanced and symmetrical, and a shoo-in for square dining rooms. A four-person table leads to relaxed conversation, as everyone has their own side and is equidistant from one another.	More than four people and you could end up with a chasm in the center that's tough to navigate.

6 picturesque place settings

Make sitting down to the meal part of the experience with tablescapes that break from routine and instantly set the mood.

blues

black + white

Turn to page 270 for information on these products.

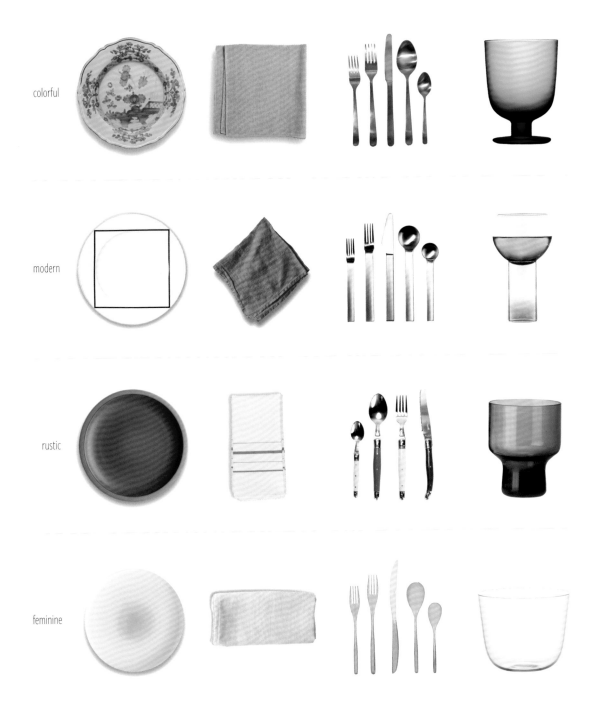

colorful

modern

rustic

feminine

setting up a spirited bar

No need for a cart on wheels. A stationary surface like a console, sideboard, or side table will work just as well. Whichever you choose, prop it with:

a few bar essentials: six bottles, at least to start; go for gin, rum, tequila, bourbon, vodka, vermouth.

decanter: you can't go wrong with crystal and a show-stopping stopper.

corkscrew, bottle opener, ice bucket, and tongs: an excellent opportunity to add thoughtful detai!. Try mother of pearl or inlaid bone for subtle glamour.

tray: a must for protecting the surface from spills.

shaker: 28 ounces is the perfect size for two drinks.

3 steps to a quick cocktail party

1. serve one signature drink Surefire winners: a classic old-fashioned, sparking wine with a fruit garnish, pimm's cup, gimlet with fresh mint.

2. offer easy-access snacks Some of our favorites: cheese and crackers, spiced nuts, picholine olives, cornichons, and crunchy crudités with a slightly spicy dipping sauce.

3. perfect your playlist Tailor tunes to match your ideal party mood: jazz, relaxed indie, a medley of Motown.

STYLE STATEMENTS

snapshots of inspiring ideas

rustic

the mood: outdoorsy, tactile, natural.

styling notes: Layers of texture—a raw wood table topped with a faux bois charger, stoneware plates, and amber glass—create a setting that feels special. The linen tea towel used as a runner unifies the disparate collection of items.

festive

the mood: warm, intimate, welcoming.

styling notes: The trimmings for a merry table can come entirely from your own backyard. Here, airy nandina berry branches and a sweet mound of red brunia in a gold bud vase speak to the striped French napkins, which are topped with greenery tied with jute. Pinecones scattered about feel at home on a weathered table. The centerpiece is a piece of driftwood topped with pine sprigs wrapped in battery-powered string lights.

striking

the mood: unique, stark, daring.

styling notes: Naturally shed pheasant feathers that match the china is a special pairing. The trompe l'oeil resin vases recall the bird's forested terrain, while polka-dotted guinea hen feathers in low cups and on each napkin subdue the starkness and play with scale.

colorful

the mood: animated, upbeat, full of life.

styling notes: This table feels like a painting; a modern vase offering big, boisterous blooms creates an intriguing preppy counterpoint. The vertically striped napkins rival the horizontal striped vase, and the swirly plates smooth out the scene. Peppering the table with a few flowers in shorter vessels creates a varied view.

casual

Mosaic tables, oversize floor pillows, and a flatweave rug all signal a loungy alfresco affair. The setup feels spontaneous, but the design is considered: Geometric patterns and unexpected color combos—dusty rose and pale blue to soften black and charcoal—elevate the look to boho-glamour status.

STYLE SCHOOL

anatomy of a cheese plate

enough for everyone
Buy 3 to 4 ounces of cheese per person, and gather five varieties—more than that will overwhelm the palate.

a trio of types
For a full range of textures and flavors, cover all three milk types—goat, cow, sheep—and experiment with different categories:

    aged (comte, cheddar)
    soft (camembert, triple creme brie)
    firm (manchego, gouda)
    blue (stilton, gorgonzola)

room temperature is best
Take cheese out of the fridge an hour before guests arrive; cold mutes the flavor.

the right knives
Use a butter knife for soft cheese and a triangular knife for hard cheese, like parmesan. Most goat and blue cheeses crumble under the knife; use a cheese wire.

carb control
Skip anything herbed or garlicky—it'll overwhelm the cheese.

perfect pairings
Choose at least one from each section:

    something sweet:
    in-season fruit; dried pears, cherries, or apricots; fig jam, raspberry preserves, apple chutney, raw honey.

    something savory:
    cornichons, olives, pickled green beans, roasted red peppers, caponata, spicy mustard.

    something meaty:
    hard salami, paper-thin prosciutto, sweet sausage bites. If you're not sure what to buy, look to your cheeses—for a French brie, consider saucisson.

    something nutty:
    Marcona almonds, shelled pistachios, walnuts.

the art of plating
Display cheese clockwise, from mild to most pungent. Be loose with your placement—sprinkle accoutrements throughout so no one has to reach too far. Labeling cheese with toothpick signs is a cute touch.

play with place settings

A crab apple cutting on each napkin mimics the sculptural central arrangement—where fruit brightens the gnarled driftwood—making the table feel like a considered tableau. The plates, with a touch of red, tie in as well.

recreate a masterpiece

Check out your fruit bowl for centerpiece inspiration. A simple plating of pears can take on the mesmerizing quality of a Cezanne still life.

cultivate a botanical landscape

Queen Anne's lace, allium, and thistles stand tall on thin, easy-to-see-through stalks that won't hinder conversation. Mismatched earthenware in muted purples, greens, and blues lends richness and depth.

10 out-of-the box serving ideas

1. Rim cocktails with chili salt.

2. Make takeout feel fancy: Serve food in porcelain bowls or pizza on cake platters.

3. Set up labeled dispensers of specially infused water: grapefruit rosemary, grape pineapple, lemon with fresh mint.

4. Create antipasto kebobs: mozzarella balls, stuffed olives, roasted peppers, artichoke hearts.

5. Prepare a vertical charcuterie board—a three-tiered platter piled high with salami, sausage, and prosciutto.

6. Toss a raspberry in each glass of Prosecco.

7. Turn dessert into decoration (shown right).

9. Let a giant serving dish steal the show.

8. Display a rainbow tomato tray with nearby sea salt and olive oil so guests can sprinkle and drizzle to their liking.

10. Make an ice mold filled with pomegranate seeds (or fresh fruit or cinnamon sticks or sprigs of herbs) to chill punch without watering it down.

ingredients for an instant cocktail party

A cocktail + two snacks = haute happy hour

Good Morning Indeed
Spicy Bloody Mary + Shrimp Cocktail + Bacon Strips

Italian Getaway
Negroni + Breadsticks + Hunk of Parmesan

Movie Night Made Better
Beer + Pizza Bagels + Chocolate-Covered Popcorn

Spanish Spread
White Sangria + Fried Calamari + Spicy Mini Meatballs

A Touch of Ginger
Dark & Stormy + Steamed Pork Dumplings + Scallion Pancakes

'60s Nostalgia
Old-Fashioned + Pigs in a Blanket + Fondue

Bubbly Essentials
Prosecco + French Fries + Dipping Sauces Galore

mood lighting

Stockpile as many white candles as you can—tapers, tea lights, pillars, the works. Stick to unscented candles, and set them on tables or low ledges rather than high shelves—you don't want anyone's hair to catch fire. Fit table and floor lamps with no higher than 25 watt bulbs, and whatever you do, switch off the harsh overheads. For outdoor gatherings, pile on the twinkle lights and grab a pretty lamp or two from inside for an unexpected glow.

timo's tips

1. Place paintings or photographs along a wall, like a gallery. This keeps the eye moving and visually tricks guests into thinking there's more space between them and the wall than actually exists.

2. A long, narrow table works well at dinner parties, (especially in a railroad apartment) and allows for more intimate conversations. Don't put it up against a wall, though—it's important that there's enough space to walk around it.

3. Alternatively, a perfectly square elevated table with high stools is an elegant way to make a room feel less cramped. (This looks great with a solid color tablecloth.)

4. Avoid clutter on a table; stick with what is being served at that moment. Family style spreads can be a mess; instead, keep all the food in the kitchen, served buffet style. For simplicity's sake, use only one course's worth of silverware.

5. Keep your table near an open window. The view can contribute to a more spacious feeling.

6. Use pared-down and simple greenery, like succulents, instead of larger floral arrangements.

7. Enhance your windows with greenery. Place a tall, lean houseplant, such as a banana leaf plant or stately cactus, next to a window to extend the feeling of spaciousness given by the view.

8. Under-lighting is a great way to enhance the height of the ceiling. Tipping a light upward creates shadows that can expand the room.

inspiring style:

timo weiland
(on small space entertaining)

Timo Weiland is the cofounder and creative director of his eponymous fashion brand. "Interiors play a large role in what we do. We are inspired by midcentury modern architecture and the American classic coastal aesthetic—an East Coast meets California style." Timo lives and plays in New York City. "I once had a party for two hundred and fifty people in a thousand-square-foot apartment," he laughs. "Entertaining in a small space has its benefits. It keeps your gatherings intimate and warm, but there is definitely a science to it."

inspiring style:

athena calderone

(on creating a stunning tablescape)

Athena Calderone, interior designer and founder of the lifestyle blog eye-swoon. com, believes her years of travel with her DJ husband and young son exposed her to diverse cultures, worked to inform her eye, and helped shape her passion for design. But ultimately it was homemaking that blossomed into her career path. "I would seek solace in the kitchen and found that experimentation, playing with different flavors and textures, became a really artful, fulfilling experience." When asked about her aesthetic, Athena says, "Simple ideas, thoughtfully executed, are best. Entertaining, making a meal, setting a beautiful table, and creating a mood are perfect ways to express your creativity."

athena's tips

1. Begin by establishing a palette: Use the seasons to inform the tone of the tablescape, as well as the menu. You might use darker, richer colors for winter, and set a light and easy tone for summer. Allow seasonal ingredients from the menu to spill onto the table. If you're preparing a blueberry dish, use clippings from blueberry bushes on the place settings.

2. Play with contrast. If you're using a mix of dark colors and gold on your table, add sprigs of greenery to counterbalance. This combination of glam and grit will give the tablescape depth. For a finishing touch, try using a chalkboard or hand-painted wooden spoons instead of name cards.

3. Instead of floral arrangements, which can get expensive and may feel too structured, rest three single blooms in a wooden bowl, or sprinkle the table with eucalyptus leaves. Add natural, organic layers to the table with fruit, such as pomegranates or lemons still attached to the branch.

4. Invest in a variety of flatware and ceramics; flea market finds are a perfect way to keep the cost down. If you buy what you love, even mismatched vintage glasses can become a one-of-a-kind collection that's unique to you.

5. Having the food prepared before your guests arrive makes entertaining easy. Place it on a sideboard or credenza and be creative with height when you plan the presentation. Use upside-down salad bowls as pedestals or pile up cork placemats to create several levels. Mix wooden platters and cutting boards with ceramic trivets to add another layer of visual interest. Add a tall vase to balance out the table or include small potted herbs, like lemon grass or tarragon, to accentuate the meal.

6. For a great conversation starter, write thoughtful quotes on small pieces of paper, roll them into scrolls, and bundle them up with twine. It's a novel way to break the ice.

shopping resources

⭐ = editors favorites v = vintage k = kid-friendly b = budget-friendly

Don't forget to check out **domino.com** for home decor finds that will help you bring *domino* style and inspiration into your home. Shop fresh ideas, current trends, and editor favorites.

WALLPAPER + FABRIC

CALICO WALLPAPER ⭐
718 243 1705
calicowallpaper.com
Taking inspiration from the marbling traditions of Japan and Turkey—as well as NASA telescope imagery—this wallpaper studio keeps things interesting with eye-catching prints like the Aurora collection.

COLE & SON ⭐
+44 (0) 208 442 8844
cole-and-son.com
Considerably bolder than you might expect from an outfit that counts the queen as a client, this British company's offerings run the gamut from exuberant nature prints to mod graphics.

COWTAN & TOUT
212 647 6900
cowtan.com
Old-fashioned and restrained, with shades of English country, the traditional prints here (including amazing florals) are sold alongside more colorful updates by designers like Manuel Canovas, whose toiles in bright oranges and pinks look anything but dowdy.

DE GOURNAY
212 564 9750
degournay.com
These incredibly lush, hand-painted papers align to create epic historical scenes or grand chinoiserie patterns, but even a single panel can remake a room.

DONGHIA
800 366 4442
donghia.com
Decorators rely on Donghia for beautifully earthy and textured papers and fabrics—we're particularly fond of its fine silks and durable outdoor textiles.

DURALEE
800 275 3872
duralee.com
Great for all of the basics, this is also a good spot to find fun prints just waiting to be discovered and used to transform a humble hand-me-down.

ESKAYEL ⭐
347 703 8084
eskayel.com
Perfectly faded graphic prints in soft blues, grays, and pinks are this environmentally minded company's signature, as well as nontoxic inks and sustainable materials like grass cloth.

FLAVOR PAPER
718 422 0230
flavorpaper.com
Featuring fire-hydrant toile and Warhol-esque bananas, everything here is lively and statement-making—and hand-printed to order, just in case you want your favorite far-out pattern in a different color. Look for their '60s- and '70s-inspired prints, which are coveted by movie set designers.

HOLLAND & SHERRY
212 355 6241
hollandsherry.com
Everything is top-notch at this respected purveyor, which started out as a tailor in 1836 and carries fabrics and wallcoverings of the highest quality, including hand-painted prints you'll want to frame.

JOHN ROSSELLI AND ASSOCIATES
212 593 2060
johnrosselliassociates.com
Those in the know trust this New York–based dealer for sublime textiles and wall coverings by Chambord Place, Twigs, and more.

JUJU PAPERS
503 764 7610
jujupapers.com
Hand-printed with playful geometrics and nature scenes, the wallpaper at Portland, Oregon based Juju (meaning "to ascribe magical powers to inanimate objects") adds a touch of whimsy to any room.

KRAVET
800 645 9068
kravet.com
The range of fabrics here is pretty dazzling, but it's the basics— simple colors, beautiful textures, and timeless styles—that keep us coming back. One stand-out: the Museum of New Mexico collection, which is adapted from the organization's archives and includes traditional patterns in saturated, earthy hues.

LEE JOFA
800 453 3563
leejofa.com
While we love all its luxe printed fabrics and wallpapers, our particular favorite at this established house is the array of archival prints.

LES INDIENNES
518 828 2811
lesindiennes.com
Created using naturally dyed cottons and traditional hand-blocking methods, Mary Mulcahy's gorgeously subtle ethnic prints are a wonderful fit in even the most minimalist interior.

MARIMEKKO k
888 308 9817
marimekko.com
Finland's iconic textile and clothing design house continues to turn out bold, bright, and classic mod prints that add character and color to any modern interior or ultra-cool kids' room.

OSBORNE & LITTLE k
212 751 3333
osborneandlittle.com
A leader in the industry since the 1960s, this London-based company reissued its debut collection of papers, which range from opulent to proper. Don't miss designer Nina Campbell's historically inspired prints or the lush botanicals from Lorca, as well as exclusive designs in bold colors from Matthew Williamson.

PIERRE FREY
212 421 0534
pierrefrey.com
This luxury house is so quintessentially French—we love the elegant traditional fabrics and wallpapers, particularly the quirky toiles.

QUADRILLE
212 753 2995
quadrillefabrics.com
The source for the China Seas collection—hand-screened prints that hover between groovily geometric and beach-house boho—Quadrille also has fun prints like Uzbek, Tropique, and the kid-friendly Peacock Batik that brighten up a room.

RAOUL TEXTILES
310 657 4931
raoultextiles.com
The color-rich, exotic, and occasionally eccentric prints here rival those found at an authentic Indian marketplace. The sky's the limit in terms of customization—for a nominal fee, you can have your print of choice custom-colored.

SCHUMACHER
800 523 1200
fschumacher.com
This storied American company's offering skews to the classic, but we're also fans of its more contemporary designs, like the aptly named Good Vibrations line featuring abstract ferns in cheerful colors.

STUDIO FOUR NYC ☆
212 475 4414
studiofournyc.com
This textile design studio boasts an eclectic inventory, including bright watercolors by Caitlin McGauley and textured florals from Ferrick Mason. Have your own designs in mind? Make an appointment with the in-house weaver to bring them to life.

SUPPLY SHOWROOM ☆
512 770 6211
supplyshowroom.com
Housed in a chic 1930s bungalow, this Austin home goods shop curates a thoughtful mix of wallpapers from small-batch studios such as Flat Vernacular and Relativity Textiles—each more eye-pleasing than the next.

WALNUT WALLPAPER ☆
323 932 9166
walnutwallpaper.com
Located in Los Angeles, Walnut specializes in unique papers by designers both indie and established. The selection of sweet, whimsical prints from Aimee Wilder, Yukari Sweeney, and Abnormals Anonymous is another draw if you're decorating a child's room.

PAINT

BEHR b
877 237 6158
behr.com
Known for high-quality stains and varnishes, Behr also excels in outdoor paints and primers.

BENJAMIN MOORE
855 724 6802
benjaminmoore.com
The gold standard for both design buffs and bright-eyed beginners, these paints go on smooth and have excellent coverage.

FARROW & BALL
888 511 1121
us.farrow-ball.com
The legendary English manufacturer is famous for its highly pigmented paints with poetically evocative names, like Borrowed Light and Setting Plaster.

PRATT & LAMBERT
800 289 7728
prattandlambert.com
Crisp colors and bright whites are the stand-outs at this more-than-a-century-old company.

RALPH LAUREN
800 379 7656
ralphlaurenpaint.com
Nobody does it like Ralph, and that includes his paint collection—a master class in stylish finishes and faux techniques like Suede, Antique Leather, and Indigo Denim.

SYDNEY HARBOUR PAINT COMPANY
310 444 2882
shpcompany.com
This small Aussie manufacturer gets its water-based paint recipes from the founder's grandfather. The colors are each hand-mixed using natural pigments for a richer hue.

FURNITURE

1ST DIBS v ☆
877 721 3427
1stdibs.com
Every one-of-a-kind gem can be found here, a dream resource for decorators thanks to the always refreshed stock of high-quality antiques and vintage pieces culled from some of the finest shops and showrooms in the US, France and England.

ANOTHER COUNTRY
+44 (0) 207 486 3251
anothercountry.com
Inspired by Shaker style, as well as traditional Scandinavian and Japanese woodworking techniques, this English outfit keeps the design spartan and the materials organic, including hardwoods, stoneware, and brass.

BAKER
800 592 2537
bakerfurniture.com
This American company offers an impressive range of shapes and styles, all elegant and handsomely tailored. We're particularly fond of designer and architect Jean-Louis Deniot's furniture collection in soft grays with hints of Art Deco.

BERNHARDT
828 313 0795
bernhardt.com
Founded in 1889, this shop maintains a crisp edit of well-designed pieces balanced with a few organic elements, such as a petrified wood side table.

CENTURY
800 852 5552

centuryfurniture.com

Century is home to an impressive
assortment of classic furnishings,
from Windsor Smith to Patrick
Aubriot, as well as an Artist in
Residence program for up-and-
coming craftspeople who develop
new work (think sculptural, layered
side tables).

CISCO BROTHERS
323 778 8612

ciscobrothers.com

The sleek inventory here keeps a
green profile: Everything is built
using sustainable wood and water-
based glues, and manufactured with
environmentally friendly processes.

DESIGN WITHIN REACH
800 944 2233

dwr.com

One-stop shopping for virtually
every modern design classic.

ETHAN ALLEN
888 324 3571

ethanallen.com

Though it excels at more traditional
pieces (including wood canopy beds
in dramatic ebony stains), we also
like some of the brand's newer, more
modern offerings, like leather sofas.

GEORGE SMITH ★
212 226 4747

georgesmith.com

Beautifully made, timelessly chic—
this is the place to find upholstered
pieces like English-style sofas and
ottomans you'll have for a lifetime.

LEE INDUSTRIES
800 892 7150

leeindustries.com

All of this eco manufacturer's
classic upholstery offerings (slipper
chairs, settees, sofas) adhere to the
company's Natural Lee standard,
which means soy-based cushions,
reclaimed-plastic backs, and water-
based finishes. We love the small-
space-friendly styles, too.

MITCHELL GOLD & BOB WILLIAMS
800 489 4195

mgbwhome.com

If you thought Gold & Williams
is only about sofas, the constantly
updated lighting and accessories
collections are also worth a look.

MODERN CONSCIENCE ✓
206 682 2443

modernconscience.com

A craftsman and a modern furniture
historian make up the duo behind
this Henry Miller–recommended
renovation studio in Seattle. They
also offer spare parts for your Womb
or Egg chair, a restoration kit (DIY-
er gift alert!) and vintage pieces
ready to be scooped up.

MODERNICA ★
323 933 0383

modernica.net

Midcentury fiends rejoice: This Los
Angeles studio churns out some
of the best reproductions around,
from George Nelson bubble lamps
to fiberglass shell chairs. You'll also
score clean-lined love seats, beds,
tables, planters, and shelves.

ROOM & BOARD
800 301 9720

roomandboard.com

This popular American retailer
offers easy, modern basics for every
room in the house, plus outdoor
and office styles. Standouts include
desks and occasional chairs.

SALVAGE ONE ✓
312 733 0098

salvageone.com

Expect the unexpected at this
Chicago-based cavernous ware-
house and events space, where you
might stumble upon an 18th-century
limestone mantel or a 1940s-style
brass and Lucite table lamp.

SERENA & LILY k ★
866 597 2742

serenaandlily.com

This California brand gets the West
Coast's effortless cool just right with
the Bungalow sofa, folding leather
stools, and other pieces for inspired
family spaces. The dedicated
Kidshop is equally well curated,
with everything from hanging
rattan chairs to luxe bedding.

VITRA
212 463 5750

vitra.com

Since 1950, this Swiss company
has manufactured furniture for
an incredible range of progressive
designers, including Charles
and Ray Eames, George Nelson,
Frank Gehry, Hella Jongerius,
and Verner Panton—in addition
to having its very own campus to
keep things current.

FLOORING

ANN SACKS
800 278 8453

annsacks.com

One of the biggest names in tile has
everything from basic penny rounds
to collections by designers like
Clodagh and Vicente Wolf.

CARLISLE WIDE PLANK
877 627 4118

wideplankflooring.com

This family business mills wide-
plank, heart-pine flooring harvested
from a 30,000-acre Alabama
plantation, and offers reclaimed
products that can all be traced to
their structure of origin.

COUNTRY FLOORS
212 627 8300

countryfloors.com

Renowned for its European
aesthetic and tiles based on 17th-,
18th-, and 19th-century designs, this
New York City–based company also
showcases beautiful natural-stone
and handmade terra-cotta options.

RUGS

AELFIE b ⭐
844 235 3437
aelfie.com
New kid Aelfie offers reasonably priced rugs that are designed in Brooklyn and handmade by artisans in India. We're also partial to the candy-colored sheepskins and hand-dyed flatweave rugs for added boho cred.

BEAUVAIS CARPETS
212 688 2265
beauvaiscarpets.com
As much an art gallery as a showroom, this spot is dedicated to fine antique rugs and equally authentic-feeling reproductions for the true connoisseur.

DASH & ALBERT
877 586 4771
dashandalbert.com
Shop for amazingly well-priced colorful patterns, plus a big range of striped and floral options.

ELSON & COMPANY
800 944 2858
elsoncompany.com
Handwoven by Tibetan weavers, the rugs here are exceptionally crafted. This San Francisco company's stock-in-trade is couture rugs by such respected names as Oscar de la Renta and Fabien Baron.

FLOR b
866 952 4093
flor.com
Welcome to environmentally responsible modular carpet tile that installs faster than wall-to-wall, goes with you when you move, and can be replaced by section if it gets stained.

LOLOI RUGS
972 503 5656
loloirugs.com
Innovative, intricate handcrafted designs at fair prices are what you can expect from this family-owned Dallas brand committed to merging craftsmanship and originality. We love the distressed designs that pair fantastically well with modern furniture.

MADELINE WEINRIB ⭐
646 602 3780
madelineweinrib.com
Textile artiste Madeline Weinrib changed the rug industry forever when she debuted her line of eye-popping, globally inspired rugs in 1997. Looking at her designs it's clear that Weinrib, also a painter, was able to find that sweet spot between brush and loom to create truly one-of-a-kind masterpieces for the floor.

MANSOUR MODERN
310 652 9999
mansourmodern.com
The many inventive, ethnic-inspired patterns at this couture shop are especially strong, but the range of designs encompasses everything from graphic looks to subdued neutrals, all of it well-made.

MERIDA MERIDIAN
800 345 2200
meridastudio.com
This is an amazing source for natural-fiber floor coverings like sea grass and sisal, jute, abaca, and beyond, all beautifully woven and bound in designs and patterns you won't see elsewhere.

OYYO ⭐
+46 76 891 19 08
oyyo.se
Working with organic cotton and vegetable dyes, this small Swedish studio uses traditional techniques to create their beautifully timeless weavings.

THE RUG COMPANY
800 644 3963
therugcompany.com
Paul Smith, Vivienne Westwood, Rodarte and other big fashion names are among the star collaborators at this site.

SAFAVIEH k
866 422 9070
safavieh.com
More on the traditional, tailored end of the spectrum, the selection here includes Thomas O'Brien's streamlined ethnic looks, along with a few statement pieces, like an animal-print rug by Jamie Drake in raspberry silk.

SHARKTOOTH v
718 451 2233
sharktoothnyc.com
If you're in the market for an antique rug, Sharktooth has you covered. The small yet eclectic collection also includes hand-dyed and patched textiles in deep indigos and grays.

STARK CARPET
844 407 8275
starkcarpet.com
It's all about the selection and quality here, from antiques to repros, Aubussons to soumaks, and brilliant custom options.

ZAK+FOX v
212 924 0199
zakandfox.com
A quirky and playful aesthetic prevails over this textiles and rugs store, started by Zak Profera and his Shiba Inu "fox" Shinji. Create your own chic clubhouse with a mid-century Tulu-style rug or "pom" print linen drapes.

LIGHTING

APPARATUS ⭐
646 527 9732
apparatusstudio.com
Sculptural pendant lights—sometimes in fanciful shapes, like the Cloud series—are the hallmark of this Manhattan duo, who also work in brass, marble, and even horsehair.

CHRISTOPHER SPITZMILLER
212 563 3030
christopherspitzmiller.com
Spitzmiller handcrafts modern lamps with classic influences in an array of colors and silhouettes.

CIRCA LIGHTING ⭐
877 762 2323
circalighting.com
With a tremendous stock of floor and table lamps, sconces and pendant lights—skewed toward the traditional, though nothing's too antique—it's no wonder this spot is so beloved by decorators.

FLOS
888 952 9541
usa.flos.com
This Italian lighting giant has collaborated with design luminaries like Philippe Starck and Patricia Urquiola, and continues to produce elegant, innovative pieces.

LINDSEY ADELMAN
212 473 2501
lindseyadelman.com
Handblown glass and locally machined metal—not to mention nautical rope and chain mail—give this Manhattan-based designer's pieces a ying/yang effect that we love.

LUMENS
877 445 4486
lumens.com
Stock up on every bulb imagin-able—whether a chrome top or a European base—at this lighting emporium.

ONE FORTY THREE b ★
702 566 8298
shop.onefortythree.com
It's hard to believe that each of the lamps on this site is individually made by a husband-wife team—for a steal, no less.

PELLE
718 243 1840
pelledesigns.com
This Brooklyn studio is a true design laboratory, where founders Jean and Oliver Pelle developed an LED light that mimics the warmth of an incandescent bulb, among other marvels.

REJUVENATION
888 401 1900
rejuvenation.com
Besides a strong collection of antique fixtures and reproductions, this company has a take-back program to ensure its products don't end up in landfills.

ROLL & HILL
718 387 6132
rollandhill.com
Find the perfect Art Deco–inspired pendant light or modern desk lamp here—a thoughtful boutique championing small-batch production and a handful of independent designers.

SCHOOLHOUSE ELECTRIC AND SUPPLY CO. b ★
800 630 7113
schoolhouseelectric.com
Past and present merge in Schoolhouse Electric's wide range of historically accurate luminaires, all of which can be hardwired to order for eco-friendly compact fluorescent lightbulbs.

THE URBAN ELECTRIC CO.
843 723 8140
urbanelectricco.com
This Charleston-based stockist collaborates closely with top design-ers (among them *domino* favorites Oro Bianco and Nickey Kehoe) on updated yet still timeless options.

WARBACH
512 522 0564
warbach.com
If you're on the hunt for a custom piece, Austin studio Warbach might be your answer. The design-build studio crafts geometric chandeliers and sconces from salvaged wood and iron for over a dozen local restaurants and residences in the Texan capital.

YLIGHTING b
866 428 9289
ylighting.com
A mega-emporium with a massive assortment of modern options in every category.

ENTERTAINING

BARNEY'S
888 222 7639
barneys.com
This favorite source for luxury goods carries gorgeous Fornasetti platters, elegant servingware, and standout pieces by hard-to-find brands like Venini.

FITZSU
323 655 1908
fitzsu.com
This couple-owned online store is a dream for hostesses and design purists alike, with entertaining essentials such as Giò Ponti flatware, Goa salad servers, and Aino Aalto glassware.

FOOD52 ★
food52.com/shop
Home to all manner of food forums and recipes from the ever-growing Food52 community, the site's equally extensive shop offering includes high-quality kitchen- and serving-ware, as well as great gifts.

GLOBAL TABLE b
212 431 5839
globaltable.com
Packed with vibrant, unusual items from around the world (all of them simple and mostly modern in design), this tiny outfit in New York's SoHo is filled with vases, tableware, and trays you won't see elsewhere.

HEATH CERAMICS ★
415 361 5552 x12
heathceramics.com
Since 1948, this West Coast establishment has turned out the distinctive hand-glazed, understated, modern work of groundbreaking artisan Edith Heath.

KNOT & BOW
718 499 0414
knotandbow.com
This Brooklyn stationery store stocks adorable party supplies. We can't get enough of the beeswax birthday candles and handmade jumbo balloons filled with confetti.

MERI MERI
650 508 2300
merimeri.com
Score sweet supplies that'll bring out the kid in you and your guests, from marbled paper napkins and paper flower cake toppers to tasseled party picks and wooden cutlery with pretty-in-pink handles.

MUD AUSTRALIA
646 590 1964
mudaustralia.com
Known for organic, timeless shapes in a calming palette of neutrals, this porcelain ceramic studio from Down Under makes each piece by hand.

PAPER SOURCE
888 727 3711
papersource.com
This is the place to personalize a party. Customize anything from place cards and cocktail napkins to coasters and favor bags, and find fun touches like fringe garland, chalkboard banners, and party hats appropriate for the older set.

SNOWE ★
888 439 9397
snowehome.com
For basics without the bore, look no further than this line of everyday essentials by Rachel Cohen and Andres Modak, who weren't thrilled by the offerings when setting up their NYC apartment, so they created their own. From white serving bowls made in Portugal to a sinuous Italian-crafted glass carafe, the wares are functional but gorgeous, and the prices (thanks to no middle man) are reasonable.

TABLEART ⭐
323 653 8278

tableartonline.com

The well-traveled owner of this high-end shop marries unexpected, little-known European and Asian lines (we're a fan of Richard Brendon's playful stripe designs) with marquee brands like Alessi and Royal Copenhagen.

WILLIAMS-SONOMA
888 922 4108

williams-sonoma.com

For every meal there is a setting at this reliable source for sophisticated and tailored goods—whether in hard-working melamine or fine French porcelain.

TEXTILES + BEDDING

ANICHINI
800 553 5309

shop.anichini.com

The luxurious textiles here run the gamut from brocade coverlets to intricate embroidered table linens, all cut and sewn by local craftswomen in an 1860 farmhouse in Tunbridge, Vermont. The company's newest offerings include ornate meditation pillows and washed-linen duvet covers.

AREA
212 924 7084

areahome.com

This design studio specializes in sleek, graphic bedding that's playful but always sophisticated.

BOLL & BRANCH ⓑ
800 678 3234

bollandbranch.com

This innovative brand prides itself on offering a completely transparent supply chain and a much lower price tag; the certified organic cotton bedding is sourced from Fair Trade farms and made in India.

BRAHMS MOUNT
800 545 9347

brahmsmount.com

One of the last remaining textile mills in the US uses antique shuttle looms to craft classic designs with a twist, like silky-smooth fine wool throws done up in ombré. You're sure to adore the rumpled-to-perfection linen towels suitable for both kitchen and bath.

CALVIN KLEIN HOME
866 513 0513

calvinklein.com

Featuring subtle patterns in a spectrum of neutrals, pastels, and earth tones, the mega-designer's linens help build a calming, casually elegant bedroom.

THE COMPANY STORE ⓑ
800 323 8000

thecompanystore.com

This Wisconsin-based outfit offers a wonderfully comprehensive selection of bedding basics in a wide range of colors, patterns, and fabrics.

FOG LINEN ⭐
617 576 1600

shop-foglinen.com

An offshoot of the Japanese line Fog Linen Work, Fog Linen carries duvet covers, blankets, and pillowcases in the brand's soft-to-the-touch linen.

FRETTE
800 353 7388

frette.com

Featuring understated design and impeccable materials, the super-luxurious linens from this storied European house are pricey but worth it.

HILL HOUSE HOME
855 244 6630

hillhousehome.com

Made in Europe using Supima cotton, this company's bedding gives a modern spin to classic linen styles—and sells crisp white PJs to match, for those wanting the complete look.

JOHN ROBSHAW TEXTILES ⓚ
212 594 6006

johnrobshaw.com

The globe-trotting designer's printed bedding is one of our absolute favorites. The hand-blocked and hand-printed patterns mix and match beautifully, and the nursery styles are unusually sophisticated.

LEONTINE LINENS ⓚ
504 899 7833

leontinelinens.com

Known for standout monograms and fine embellishments, these luxurious handmade linens can be customized to your exact specifications.

LIBECO
+32 051 484851

libecohomestores.com

With different collections named after romantic locales like Notting Hill and Brick Lane, this Belgian linen line has that slightly scruffy Euro sensibility we love.

MATOUK
855 795 7600

matouk.com

Family-run since 1929, this old-school American brand now collaborates with modern talents but still offers traditional touches like custom colors and monograms.

MATTEO ⭐
213 617 2813

matteohome.com

Simple in design but made from luxurious natural materials, this LA-made bedding has a modern rustic (but not too country) chic.

OLATZ

212 255 8627

olatz.com

A favorite of high-end designers, Olatz Schnabel's super-indulgent linen-and-cotton sheets boast bold color combinations and elaborate hand-embroidered details.

PARACHUTE ♭ ☆

855 888 5977

parachutehome.com

We love that this brand's Egyptian and Turkish cotton bedding is certified chemical- and synthetic-free—as well as the fact that it partners with a U.N. organization to donate malaria bed nets.

SOCIETY

societylimonta.com

This Italian company approaches bedding like fashion, experimenting with textile processes and mix-and-match color palettes to create "couture" for the home.

HARDWARE + FIXTURES

BARBER WILSONS & CO. ☆

800 727 6317

barberwilsons.com

Traditional kitchen and bathroom faucets of the highest quality distinguish this British institution, the sole supplier for Queen Elizabeth II and such top London hotels as Claridge's, The Savoy, and The Dorchester.

DORNBRACHT

800 774 1181

dornbracht.com

The rigorously sleek, architectural hardware for kitchen and bath from this German manufacturer never forsakes functionality. (Hint: Your contractor can buy this company's products for you.)

DURAVIT

888 387 2848

duravit.us

Duravit excels at creating an ultra-clean look that doesn't leave you cold. Check out the Delos and Scola styles.

E.R. BUTLER & CO. ☆

617 722 0230

erbutler.com

This high-end American manufacturer lovingly handcrafts a wide range of traditional and custom hardware and produces designs by such luminaries as Ted Muehling.

GROHE

800 444 7643

grohe.com/us

Europe's largest faucet manufacturer specializes in forward-thinking aesthetics and technological innovation.

KOHLER ☆

800 456 4537

us.kohler.com

Family-owned since 1873, this great American outfit has everything—all of it incredibly well-made.

THE NANZ COMPANY

212 367 7000

nanz.com

Each of the finely crafted high-end hinges, knobs, and pulls from this five-person atelier is truly beautiful, and the custom pieces are works of art.

NEWPORT BRASS ♭

949 417 5207

newportbrass.com

Conscientious decorators rely on the epic inventory at this affordable kitchen and bath depot. Two of our favorites: the East Square and Miro lines.

P.E. GUERIN INC.

212 243 5270

peguerin.com

The handiwork of this venerable family business—going strong since 1857—can be seen in historic homes around the US. If money's no object, indulge in the painstakingly crafted hardware.

RESTORATION HARDWARE

800 762 1005

restorationhardware.com

Solid customer service and reasonable prices make Restoration a trusty spot for finding modern and vintage designs with unique details, like glossy black glass knobs.

ROHL

800 777 9762

rohlhome.com

Artisanal craftsmanship (e.g., faucets that riff on Edwardian and Georgian architecture), plus the sublime "Modern" line make this brand, launched in 1983, feel older than it is.

SIMON'S HARDWARE & BATH

888 274 6667

simons-hardware.com

This popular Manhattan showroom contains an impressive range of hardware and fixtures, from tiny minimalist hooks to grand old-fashioned tubs.

SUNRISE SPECIALTY ☆

510 729 7277

sunrisespecialty.com

This decades-old company carefully crafts authentic reproductions of Victorian-era bathware, including a huge range of cast-iron tubs and faucets, hand showers, and tubfills.

SUPERFRONT

+46 8 68 44 18 14

superfront.com

Taking Ikea hack to the next level, this Swedish company makes sleek handles in leather and brass, tops in materials like Carrara marble, and other design-minded details to elevate your Ikea pieces.

URBAN ARCHEOLOGY

212 371 4646

urbanarchaeology.com

The storied New York destination offers a well-edited selection of stylish lighting, hardware, washstands, and freestanding tubs.

WATERWORKS ☆

800 899 6757

waterworks.com

An established player in the pricey-but-worth it category, Waterworks carries top styles like the Aero and Enfield lines, as well as the handsome R.W. Atlas collection.

WHITECHAPEL LTD. ♭

800 468 5534

whitechapel-ltd.com

A mind-boggling assortment of kitchen hardware fills this impressively organized website, from reproduction cabinet pulls to modern hinges to graceful latches.

PLANTS + OUTDOOR LIVING

ARCHITECTURAL POTTERY
858 385 1960
architecturalpottery.com
Launched in 1950, this company delivers exactly what the name suggests: custom-made planters and garden accessories in clean, sculptural forms with choose-your-own colors and finishes.

JAMALI GARDEN b
201 869 1333
jamaligarden.com
This unexpectedly amazing party resource offers strings of lights and floral designers' tools, as well as votive candles by the dozen for setting the perfect outdoor fête.

LIGHT & LADDER
401 241 9527
lightandladder.com
Ceramic and leather hanging planters, porcelain bud vases, and elegant accessories like the slim-necked watering vessels are some of the highlights at this Brooklyn-based studio.

LOLL DESIGNS
877 740 3387
lolldesigns.com
A leader in designing with recycled plastic, this company carries durable outdoor furniture in geometric shapes and a bright palette.

THE SILL b ★
thesill.com
A one-stop-(online) shop for all things botanical, from ferns potted in brightly colored vessels to succulent starter kits, this user-friendly site also offers tips and how-tos for aspiring green thumbs.

SPROUT HOME ★
718 388 4440
shop.sprouthome.com
Locations in Chicago and Brooklyn give urbanites a much-needed nature fix. Small-space solutions abound, from hanging glass terrariums and macrame plant hangers to mini planters perfect for windowsills.

STEEL LIFE
shopsteellife.com
This store's small but considered collection includes midcentury-style vessels in powder-coated steel and plant stands in walnut. For something extra-unique, you can also go the custom-made route.

TERRAIN ★
877 583 7724
shopterrain.com
A comprehensive source for gardening and outdoor living, Terrain stocks everything you might need for the patio, greenhouse, balcony, and beyond—and gets that lightly weathered look just right.

SMALL HOME GOODS

A.G. HENDY & CO. HOME STORE HASTINGS v
+44 (0) 1424 447171
aghendy.com/homestore
The online home to the lovingly restored London townhouse of the same name offers heirloom-quality goods, both new and vintage, chosen by founder and all-around-creative type Alastair Hendy.

THE CITIZENRY
866 356 4284
the-citizenry.com
"Homegoods with a soul and a story" is how The Citizenry describes its wares—and each item is presented in terms of where and how it was made, from graphic baskets handwoven in Uganda to foldable leather lounge chairs crafted in Argentina.

HAWKINS NEW YORK ★
844 469 3344
hawkinsnewyork.com
Artisanal know-how meets effortless chic at this homewares shop, where you can pick up the essentials—Moroccan water glasses, linen pillows, oak cutting boards—along with a few key pieces, like their popular Grady Ladder.

JENNI KAYNE
310 695 1223
jennikayne.com
Easy breezy California living defines this designer's simple, tailored sensibility. Her curated selection of home wares includes cloth dish covers as an alternative to plastic wrap and white ceramic jingle bells by Michele Quan.

JOINERY ★
347 889 6164
joinerynyc.com
Purveyor of the famed Eagle and Diamond blankets in minimalist patterns, Joinery is your go-to for well-crafted treasures, like a Pioneer chair or festive papier-maché mobile.

LABOUR AND WAIT
+44 (0) 207729 6253
labourandwait.co.uk
Enduring classics reign supreme at this London outpost. Frustrated by constantly redesigning clothing for ever-changing trends, founders Rachel Wythe-Moran and Simon Watkins changed courses, curating a line of home wares fit for the ages. Think galvanized buckets with wooden handles and enamel soap dishes.

LEIF k
leifshop.com
Happy-making home accents and style accessories in fun prints and refreshing colors—a polka-dot tray here, a pom-pom basket there—keep us coming back for more.

THE LINE
646 678 4908
theline.com
This on-point style source tailors an equally sharp selection for the home, including books, candles, and other small luxuries that make the most thoughtful housewarming gifts.

LOST & FOUND k
various locations
lostandfoundshop.com
This Hollywood mainstay, which has since branched out to Santa Monica, is an emporium for refined yet unfussy goods, with something for every taste and budget.

MICHAEL TRAPP v
860 672 6098

shopmichaeltrapp.com

If you're in search of something truly rare, look to Michael Trapp, whose antiques collection spans several centuries and includes a veritable cabinet of curiosities.

MOMA STORE k
800 851 4509

momastore.org

Every design-lover's happy place, the MoMA store is the source for modern classics and collectibles that merge clever with functional, including books, lighting, accessories, kitchenware, and office supplies.

MUJI b
muji.com

Everything at this design-minded Japanese retailer is a practical yet fun purchase, whether a craft-paper notebook or a glass teapot.

NALATA NALATA
212 228 1030

nalatanalata.com

You can feel the care that went into choosing each item at this shop, where the husband-wife team focuses on everyday Japanese goods that aim to delight.

NANNIE INEZ ★
512 428 6639

nannieinez.com

An Austin fixture, this concept shop prides itself on carrying hard-to-find pieces from around the world—at reasonable prices.

NICKEY KEHOE ★
323 954 9300

nickeykehoe.com

Todd Nickey and Amy Kehoe, interior designers and arbiters of good taste, lead this Los Angeles studio full of accessories like Japanese ceramic bud vases, powder-coated steel waste bins, African seagrass baskets, and cast-iron bookends.

OROBORO
718 388 4884

oroborostore.com

East and West coast converge at this Brooklyn boutique, which stocks ceramic wall hangings, traditional woven hammocks, quilted throw pillows, and other must-haves for the modern boho.

POKETO k
213 537 0751

poketo.com

Cheerful colors and smart, playful designs make this small-goods purveyor the retail equivalent of a pick-you-up.

SPARTAN ★
505 600 1015

spartan-shop.com

The name says it all: This site is for lovers of design distilled to the most essential, with a focus on natural materials and rich textures.

STEVEN ALAN HOME k
877 978 2526

stevenalan.com/home-store

Hand-thrown mugs, scented soaps, organic cotton towels, and other necessities round out the clothing brand's understated home offerings.

UMBRA b
800 387 5122

umbra.com

From hooks, shelves, and storage to barware and kitchen tools, you'll find them all here in streamlined Modern shapes and at budget-friendly prices

EVERYTHING FOR THE HOME

ABC CARPET & HOME v ★
212 473 3000

abchome.com

This one-of-a-kind mega-emporium is stocked with treasures old and new (many of them eco-friendly) from the most remote points on the globe. Look for the world's comfiest sofas, a well-vetted bedding selection, and, of course, a rug oasis across the street.

AMARA
866 896 3804

us.amara.com

In addition to carrying high-end brands like Mulberry Home and Tom Dixon, this smartly curated UK site also develops its own line of home furnishings and accessories.

ANTHROPOLOGIE
800 309 2500

anthropologie.com

This favorite has perfected a gently worn bohemian aesthetic that's reflected in everything from elegant sofas to small decorative accessories.

CB2 b
800 606 6252

cb2.com

The modern and budget-conscious little sister of Crate & Barrel, CB2 is great for small-space furniture and fun accents.

THE CONRAN SHOP ★
+44 116 269 1083

conranshop.co.uk

From vintage to modern and everything in between, this design institution, founded by English designer Terence Conran in 1974, is always on point.

CRATE & BARREL
800 967 6696

crateandbarrel.com

Handsome and solidly built, this mass retailer's furniture line keeps things fresh with of-the-moment styles and palettes.

THE FUTURE PERFECT ★
877 388 7373

thefutureperfect.com

Once a modest shopfront in Brooklyn, this design emporium has expanded to include a whole array of housewares. We love their clever accents, like trompe l'oeil wallpaper and brass paperweights.

H.D. BUTTERCUP v
310 558 8900

hdbuttercup.com

More than 50 top furniture manufacturers offer everything from oriental carpets to luxury mattresses here—minus any middleman prices.

HORNE
877 404 6763

shophorne.com

Enduring design underlies every piece at Horne, a favorite of architects and interior designers for its spirited and eclectic selection.

IKEA b
800 434 4532

ikea.com

Though the catalog might be easier to navigate than the massive stores, no one does inexpensive, on-point design like Ikea.

JAYSON HOME v
800 472 1885

jaysonhome.com

This superstore has a comprehensive stock of classic furniture and accessories, plus excellent vintage finds and a well-stocked garden section.

JOHN DERIAN COMPANY v ★
800 677 3207

johnderian.com

Best known for his whimsical decoupage work, John Derian also stocks textiles, candles, and small furniture, along with lifelike marble fruit, hand-painted wooden books, and other wonderfully imaginative gifts.

JONATHAN ADLER k
800 963 0891

jonathanadler.com

Adler turns out a line of fun, glamorous furniture, lamps, mirrors, and more in his signature jewel tones and punchy patterns.

LAYLA GRACE k
626 356 2133

laylagrayce.com

A home store with a dreamy, feminine aesthetic (think rose quartz bowls, botanical framed prints, and silk-linen comforters), Layla Grace also carries bedding and furniture for kids.

LEKKER HOME
877 753 5537

lekkerhome.com

An unfussy approach to design with an emphasis on natural materials is what defines this Boston-based retailer, which has lesser-known brands, such as English furniture-maker Ercol, along with the bigger names.

MANUFACTUM
+49 2309 939 095

manufactum.com

You can find everything imaginable at this stockist (a home goods giant in Germany), as well as some marvelously old-fashioned items, like a folding linen travel bag and leather doorstopper.

MATTER
212 343 2600

mattermatters.com

Forward-thinking manufacturer and showroom Matter bills itself as a platform for design as much as a shop—and with its impeccable who's who of designers both established (Enzo Mari, Zaha Hadid) and emerging (resident studio designer Ana Kras), we agree.

MENU ★
+45 48 40 6100

store.menudesignshop.com

For the minimalist, Menu is a haven for simple, considered design with a Scandinavian feel (many of the designers hail from Europe).

MERCI ★
+33 (0)1 80 05 29 67

merci-merci.com

In Paris's historic Haut-Marais district lies a bazaar that doesn't want to be one thing, it wants to be everything: The mix of home goods are traditional and contemporary, low-end and high-brow, one-of-a-kind and mass-produced. From an edgy slipcovered armchair to an exposed-bulb clamp light to pre-washed linen napkins, the offerings have an irresistible European sensibility and are designed to delight.

MODISH STORE
888 542 0111

modishstore.com

"Clean" design at this online retailer means streamlined shapes and sustainable practices, including a section dedicated to using reclaimed and recycled materials.

NORMANN COPENHAGEN b
+45 35 55 44 59

normann-copenhagen.com

Accessible Danish design with prices to match make this a favorite for scoring on-trend pieces to instantly update your space.

RUBY BEETS ★
631 899 3275

rubybeets.com

The new and vintage stock at this Long Island mainstay includes muslin-upholstered George Sherlock sofas and Holmegaard glassware—as well as finishing touches like handwoven baskets, sculptural lamps, and photography prints.

WEST ELM
888 922 4119

westelm.com

Head to West Elm for elegant basics, from perfectly proportioned Parsons tables to design-forward storage pieces to well-made picture frames in modern materials.

WORLD MARKET b
877 967 5362

worldmarket.com

These souk-like spaces are packed with handmade furniture and smaller items from exotic locales—all of it very affordable.

ART

ART STAR b ★
888 488 757

artstar.com

This genius site serves as your very own e-curator by custom printing, framing, and authenticating works by emerging contemporary artists that are then delivered right to your doorstep.

CLIC ★
212 966 2766

clic.com

With locations in New York, St. Barth and the Hamptons, Clic carries a chic selection of contemporary photography, travel and fashion books, as well as small home goods, to match its nomadic roots.

LARSON JUHL
800 438 5031

larsonjuhl.com

From molding to matboard, modern to vintage-inspired, Larson Juhl is a trusted expert for framing your latest finds.

MASCOT STUDIO
212 228 9090

mascotstudio.com

An East Village cornerstone since 1982, Mascot offers custom and pre-made frames that exude character—much like the space, which owner and artist Peter McCaffrey decorates with his famed doggie portraits and other work by local artists.

PICTURE ROOM b ★
212 219 2789
goodsforthestudy.mcnally-
jacksonstore.com
Around the corner from New
York's McNally Jackson Books, this
smartly organized space sells "goods
to enrich your study practice"—
whether that be a handsome brass
paperweight or sleek ballpoint.

MINTED k
888 828 6468
minted.com
An amazing array of customizable
options (not to mention a covetable
children's art section) makes
Minted our go-to for gifts and
special occasions—order a line
drawing of your home or frame your
favorite quote.

PACE PRINTS
paceprints.com
A quick glance at the roster of
artists here—Sol LeWitt, Kiki
Smith, Ed Ruscha—will have you
measuring every inch of empty
space on your walls. Plus, Pace's
masterful printmaking techniques,
such as woodcut and photogravure,
make their works even more
unique.

PADDLE8 v
212 343 1142
paddle8.com
Bid on one-of-a-kind pieces, from
museum-quality contemporary art
to of-the-moment design objects,
through this online auction house.

PATRICK PARRISH v
212 219 9244
patrickparrish.com
Curator, collector, and artist Patrick
Parrish has a sixth sense for finding
and exhibiting promising new talent
at his New York space, as well as
sourcing great midcentury pieces.

RIFLE PAPER CO. b
407 622 7679
riflepaperco.com
Pick up a graphic botanical print,
tapestry-stitched notebook, toile
gift wrap, and other flights of
fancy (temporary gold floral tattoo,
anyone?) at this fine paper purveyor.

SOCIAL PRINT STUDIO b
socialprintstudio.com
Want to turn your photos into a
book? How about a large-format
print on glossy Kodak paper? This
friendly printing service transforms
your best shots into works of art.

TAPPAN ★
213 226 6452
tappancollective.com
The place "where today's best
emerging artists meet their
collectors," Tappan takes pride in
carefully selecting each work—
without charging you the steep
gallery markup. We especially love
Claire Oswalt's abstract watercolor
collages in soft blues and grays.

WINDOWS + TREATMENTS

CHATEAU DOMINGUE
713 961 3444
chateaudomingue.com
In addition to the low-profile,
streamlined metal windows and
doors that founder Ruth Gay fell
for while traveling through Europe,
this company imports reclaimed
roof tiles, arches, columns, and
gates, along with antique lights
and mirrors.

THE SHADE STORE b
800 754-1455
theshadestore.com
This family-run business assembles
made-to-order Roman shades,
custom drapes, and other stylish
treatments (look for their exclusive
designer fabric collaborations)
directly in their workshop.

THE SILK TRADING CO. ★
323 954 9280
silktrading.com
Carrying much more than the
name suggests, this Los Angeles
house features custom window
treatments in velvet, mohair,
leather, cotton, and more. Ready-
made drapes are also available
through the Drapery-Out-of-a-Box
line, featuring their best-selling
designs for less.

SMITH & NOBLE b
888 214 2134
smithandnoble.com
From a simple café curtain to
Parisian pleat drapes, Smith &
Noble offers everything you might
need—as well as in-home design
consultations to get started.

INDEX

PRODUCT CREDITS

p. 6: Eskayel Madagascar Rose; p. 8: Flat Vernacular To & Fro – Madeleine; p. 26 (from top): Schumacher Couleur Force Leather, Schumacher Chester Wool in Pistachio, Waterhouse Jermyn Street Check in Black Oyster, Peter Fasano Delta Linen in Thatch, Studio Four NYC Fayyaz, China Seas Fez Background; p. 32 (clockwise from top): First Rocking Chair valerie-objects.com/Photo: Fien Muller, De La Espada Blanche Bergère, Acapulco Chair innitdesigns.com; p. 33 (clockwise from top left): Ballard Designs Louisa Bergère Chair, Armchair 41 Paimio by Alvar Aalto for Artek, Oomph Raffia Slipper Chair, Knoll Bertoia Diamond Chair; p. 54 (from top): Astek Inc. Submerged Anemone Shell, Pierre Frey Kazoo, Cole & Son Woodgrain Black & White, Schumacher Feather Bloom, Nobilis Brazilia; p. 108 (from top): PID Floors Oak, PID Floors American Walnut, Aronson's Floor Covering, Imports from Marrakesh Eight Point Star, Waterworks Concourse Field Tile Concrete, The Home Depot Winteron Oak Laminate Flooring; p. 110 (from top): Tibetano, Madeline Weinrib Dhurrie Ditto Blue, Aronson's Floor Covering Abaca, Ernest Outdoor Rug; p. 129: notonthehighstreet.com (top left), FLOR/Bruce Quist (top right); p. 234: Tiina the Store Indigo 10" plate, CB2 Indigo Stripe Napkins, Goa Cutlery White Handle – Brushed Stainless Steel by Cutipol for Horne, Iittala Kastehelmi Tumbler (top row), notNeutral Constellation Plate, Alfred Collection Grid Napkin by photographer Ben Kist for MARCH www.marchsf.com, CB2 Matte Black Flatware, Lobmeyr Series "B" Champagne Glass (middle row), Richard Ginori Oriente Italiano Porpora Dinner Plate, Canvas Home Oslo Cutlery Set in Matte Gold, Lempi Glass Lilac by Iittala for Horne (bottom row); p. 235: Continental Flatware Set by Gourmet Settings, Tulip Tall Glass by Fferrone Design for Horne (top

row), Heath Rim Line Dinner Plate/ Photo: Jeffery Cross, Heather Taylor Home Sand Napkins 4, Brookfarm General Store 24 Piece Flatware Set – Linen, Nouvel Studio Cura Glass (middle row), Nikko Ceramics Cloud Dinner Plate, Brookfarm General Store Large Washed Linen Napkin – Rose, Sambonet "Bamboo" 5-piece Place Setting, Lobmeyr Glass Pink Cocktail Tumbler (bottom row)

Get the Look: Midcentury

p. 31 (clockwise from top left): Saarinen Dining Table, Knoll; Nelson Bubble Lamp Criss Cross Saucer Pendant designed by George Nelson/Photo: dwell.com; Courtesy of Phaidon Press, www.phaidon.com; Marble Two Arm Candlesticks by Chen Chen and Kai Williams for The Future Perfect/Photo: Lauren Coleman; Eames Molded Plywood Lounge Chair Designed by Charles and Ray Eames for Herman Miller/Photo: Courtesy Herman Miller, Inc., Source: Herman Miller, store.hermanmiller.com; Flower Bottle, Clamlab/Photo: Clair Catillaz; Reese Sheepskin Rug in Off-White, Safavieh

Get the Look: Rustic

p. 61 (clockwise from top left): Heath Ceramics Medium Covered Serving Dish in Aqua/Photo: Jeffery Cross; Lostine Large Rolling Pin/Photo: Jason Varney; Oil Decanter 2 by Gentner Design for Horne; Kaufman Mercantile Black Walnut Trencher Board; WorkOf Todo Bien Chair, www.workof.com Photo: West of Noble/Brookfarm General Store Copper Measuring Cups; Wrap Decanter by Simon Hasan for Horne

Get the Look: Graphic

p. 89 (clockwise from top center): Louise Gray Throw Quilt No. 1/Photo: Lee Stanford Photography; Winkel 127 Table Lamp - One Arm by Wastberg for Horne; Hayley Reagan for ArtStar; L.L. Bean Pima Cotton Percale Sheet, Windowpane; Champ Stool by

Visibility for Matter Made

Get the Look: Scandinavian

p. 121 (clockwise from top left): Schoolhouse Electric & Supply Co. Luna Pendant; Omero 19th Century Swedish Farmhouse Table; Eames Molded Plastic Side Chair with Wire Base Designed by Charles and Ray Eames for Herman Miller/Photo: Courtesy Herman Miller, Inc., Source: Herman Miller, store.hermanmiller. com; Norman Copenhagen Folk Candlestick Tray in Light Blue; Toss Around by Kibisi for Muuto; New Norm Dinnerware Starter Set by Norm Architects for Dwell

Get the Look: Serene

p. 143 (clockwise from top left): ©Steidl; A Question of Eagles Large Zig Zag Vase, jennikayne.com; Rip by John Hogan, Photo: Lauren Coleman; Lindsay Cowles "White on White," Deborah Ehrlich Medium Bowl, Retail location: Barneys.com & select Barneys New York stores; Christiane Perrochon White Beige Large Centerpiece Vase/Photo: Ben Kist for MARCH; Victoria Morris Pottery

Get the Look: Cottage

p. 195 (clockwise from top left): Loom Decor's Walk the Line Throw Pillow in Blueberry; Eskayel "Splash" in Cerulean; Brahms Mount Cotton Herringbone Throw with Hand Twisted Fringe - White/Cornsilk; Wisteria Colonial Column Side Table, www.wisteria.com; Hedgehouse Majorca Throwbed in Charcoal; Serena & Lily Pondicherry Headboard

PHOTO/DESIGNER CREDITS

Illustrations: Kaarina Mackenzie
p 10: Nicole Franzen/Christene Barberich; p. 13: Amber Ulmer/Hey Wanderer; p. 15 (clockwise from top left): Molly Winters/Claire Zinnecker, Nathan Kirkman/Graham Kostic & Fran Taglia, James Waddell, Domino/ Dekar Designs, Domino/Anne Ziegler, Domino/Nate Berkus Associates, Molly Winters; p. 17: Bows & Arrows Gemma Ingalls; p. 19: Joy Sohn; p. 20: Domino/Julia Leach; p. 22: Derek Swalwell (left), Nicole Franzen/ Christene Barberich (right); p. 23: Laure Joliet/Frances Merrill (top), Domino/Ariel Ashe (bottom); p. 24: Domino/Katie Lee; p. 25: Nicole Franzen/Christene Barberich; p. 27: Domino/Ali Cayne; p. 28: Melanie Acevedo (left), Domino (right); p. 29: Nathan Kirkman/Graham Kostic & Fran Taglia; p. 31: James Waddell; p. 34: Robert Peterson of Rustic White Photography/Mandy Kellogg Rye of MKR Design; p. 35: Anna Wolf/ Rebecca Omweg (left), Mia Baxter Smail/Maya Nairn (right); p. 36: Domino/Ali Cayne (left), Matt Albiani (right); p. 37: Patrick Cline/Kate Schelter (left), Domino (right); p. 38: Domino (left), Tiffany Haynes (right); p. 39 (from top): Michael Newsted, Bonnie Tsang; p. 40: Paul Costello (left), Michael Wiltbank (right); p. 41: Tessa Neustadt/Amber Lewis; pp. 42–43: Amy Neunsinger/Rebecca De Ravenel; pp. 44–45: Jenny Gage + Tom Betterton/Aurora James; p. 46: Domino/Katie Martinez; p. 48: Domino; p. 49: Domino/Jen Smith; p. 50: Amy Bartlam/Natalie Myer; p. 51–53: Laure Joliet/Frances Merrill; p. 55: Frances Tulk-Hart; p. 56: Laure Joliet/Frances Merrill; p. 57: Ellie Cashman Design Dark Floral; p. 58: Nathan Kirkman/Graham Kostic & Fran Taglia (left), Domino/Nate Berkus Associates (right); p. 59: Domino/ Andréa Krueger (left), Domino (right); p. 60: Laure Joliet/Jenni Kayne; p. 61 (bottom right): matdesign24/iStock Photo; pp. 62–63: Mia Baxter Smail/

Sarah Wittenbraker; p. 64: Domino/ Julia Leach; p. 65: Laure Joliet/Jenni Kayne; p. 66: Domino/Ron Marvin (left), Laure Joliet/Frances Merrill (right); p. 67: Courtesy of Domino; p. 68: Domino/Lauren Leiss; p. 69: Miguel Flores-Vianna; p. 70: Domino/ Anna Burke; p. 71 (clockwise from top left): Domino/John and Christine Gachot, Molly Winters, David Black; p. 72: Gaelle Le Boulicaut (left), Manolo Yllera/Amaya De Toledo (right); p. 73: Domino/Heather Taylor; pp. 74–75: Laure Joliet/Barbara Bestor; p. 76: Wing Ta/Kate Arends; p. 78: Domino/Maryam Nassirzadeh (left), Frances Tulk-Hart (right); p. 79: Joy Sohn/Eddie Lee; p. 80: Domino/ Lauren Leiss; p. 81: Molly Winters; p. 83: Domino/Kristen Giorgi & Laura Naples; p. 84: Domino/Milly De Cabrol (left), Domino/Julia Leach (right); p. 85: Domino/Ariel Ashe (left), Domino (right); p. 86: Domino (left), Domino/ Lauren Leiss (right); p. 87: Domino/ Sally King Benedict (top), Domino (bottom); p. 88: Domino/Ariel Ashe; pp. 90–91: Patrick Cline/Kate Schelter; p. 92: Domino; p. 93: Mia Baxter Smail/ Maya Nairn (top), Laure Joliet/Jenni Kayne (bottom); p. 94: Max Kim-Bee; p. 95: Domino/Maryam Nassirzadeh (left), Ashley Gieseking/Amie Corley (right); p. 96–97 (from left): Michael Rubenstein/Brittany S. Chevalier, Domino/Jenni Li, Robert Peterson/ Brian Patrick Flynn, Amy Neunsinger/ Rebecca De Ravenel, Nathan Kirkman/Graham Kostic & Fran Taglia, Laure Joliet/Frances Merrill; p. 98: Domino/Hayley Sarno & Patrick Mele (left), Domino/Nate Berkus Associates (right); p. 99: William Abranowicz; pp. 100–102: Nathan Kirkman/Graham Kostic & Fran Taglia; p. 104: Lucas Allen (left), Amy Neunsinger/Lily Ashwell (right); p. 105: Robert Peterson; p. 106: Domino/Jenny Komenda; p. 107: Melanie Acevedo; p. 109: Domino/Heather Taylor; p. 111: Domino; p. 112: Jack Coble; p. 114: Tessa Neustadt/Ben & Jolene Kraus; p. 115: Domino/Anna Burke (left), Paul

Costello (right); p. 116: Domino/Jen Smith; p. 117: Domino; p. 118: Domino/ Sacha Dunn; p. 119: Mikkel Vang (left), Molly Winters (right); p. 120: Domino/ Anne Ziegler; p. 122: Domino/Lynn K. Leonidas (left), Domino/Anna Burke (right); p. 123: Domino/Suzanne and Lauren McGrath (top), Max Kim-Bee/ Jonathan Greenwood (bottom); p. 124–125: Domino/Maryam Nassirzadeh; p. 126: Melanie Acevedo (left), Domino/ Jenni Li (right); p. 126: Domino/Patrick Mele (left), Michael Wiltbank (right); p. 128: Melanie Acevedo/Chassie Post; p. 129 (bottom): Justin Bernhaut; pp. 130–131: Alyssa Rosenheck/Elsie Larson; p. 132: Laura Resen; p. 134: Melanie Acevedo; p. 135: Joy Sohn; p. 136: Christian Oth/Henry & Co. Design; p. 137: Domino/Anne Ziegler (left), Nathan Kirkman/Graham Kostic & Fran Taglia (right); p. 139: Annie Schlechter; p. 140: Nathan Kirkman/ Graham Kostic & Fran Taglia (left), Laure Joliet/Jenni Kayne (right); p. 141: Annie Schlechter (left), Domino (right); p. 142: Domino/Anne Ziegler; pp. 144–145: Alyssa Rosenheck/Lori Paranjape; p. 146: Domino/Ali Cayne; p. 147: Shades of Blue Interiors; p. 148: Lindsey Orton Photography/House of Jade Interiors; p. 149: Domino/ Austyn Zung; p. 150: Veronique Rautenberg (top), Ditte Isager (bottom); p. 151: Domino; p. 152: Joy Sohn; p. 154: Domino/Jenny J Norris (left), Domino (right); p. 155: Wing Ta/Kate Arends (top), Laure Joliet/Elise Joseph (bottom); pp. 156–157 (from left): Joy Sohn/Joana Avillez, Melanie Acevedo, Justin Bernhaut, Michael Wiltbank, Pia Ulin/Ulla Johnson, Michael Wiltbank; pp. 158–159: Molly Winters; p. 160: Domino/Katie Martinez; p. 162: Justin Bernhaut; p. 163: Werner Straube Photography; p. 164: Molly Winters; p. 165: Domino/Benjamin Vandiver; p. 167: Ashley Capp; p. 168: Nathan Kirkman/Graham Kostic & Fran Taglia (left), Nancy Neil (right); pp. 169–171: Molly Winters; pp. 172–173: Wing Ta/Kate Arends; p. 174: Domino/ Ron Marvin (left), Sara Kerens/Brynn

Elliott Watkins (right); p. 175: Domino (left), Sean Litchfield/Chango & Co. (right); p. 176: Domino/Lauren Leiss (left), Pia Ulin/Ulla Johnson (right); p. 177: Armelle Habib; pp. 178–179 (from left): Simon Upton, Douglas Friedman, Nancy Neil, Domino/ Jenny Komenda; pp. 180–181: Matthew Williams; p. 182: Domino/Jen Smith; p. 184: Mikkel Vang; p. 185: Laure Joliet/ Jenni Kayne; p. 186: Domino/Anne Ziegler; p. 187: Domino/Chay Wike; p. 188–190: Domino; p. 191 (clockwise from top left): Pia Ulin/Ulla Johnson, Joy Sohn/Eddie Lee, Nicole Franzen/ Christene Barberich; p. 192: Domino; p. 193: Simon Upton (top), Alyssa Rosenheck/Lori Paranjape (bottom); p. 194: Max Kim-Bee; p. 195: High Impact Photography/iStock Photo (bottom left); p. 196: Joy Sohn (left), Patrick Cline/Kate Schelter (right); p. 197: Paul Costello; p. 198: Alyssa Rosenheck/Lori Paranjape (left), Mia Baxter Smail/ Maya Nairn (right); p. 199: Domino/ Anne Ziegler; p. 200: Amy Bartlam/ Natalie Myers (left), Pia Ulin/Ulla Johnson (top right), Michael Wiltbank (bottom right); p. 201: Domino; pp. 202–203: Laure Joliet/Frances Merrill; p. 204: Eve Wilson; p. 206: Joy Sohn; p. 207: Domino; p. 208: Max Kim-Bee; p. 209: Domino/Katie Martinez; p. 214: Molly Winters (left), Douglas Friedman (right); p. 215: Patrick Cline/ Kate Schelter (top), Miguel Flores-Vianna; p.p. 216–217: Gemma Ingalls; p. 218: Mikkel Vang (left), Domino/ Ariel Ashe (right); p. 219: Gemma Ingalls. Deborah Jaffe (right); p. 220: April Valencia/Taylor Patterson; p. 221: Ryan Flynn Photography; pp. 222–223 (from left): Domino/Paloma Contreras, Gately Williams, Sarah Elliott/Dekar Design, Francesco Lagnese, Gemma Ingalls; pp. 224–225: Michael Wiltbank; p. 226: Domino/Heather Taylor; p. 228: Jessica Isaac; p. 229: Beth Kirby; p. 230: Michael Wiltbank; p. 231: Gemma Ingalls; p. 233: Alyssa Rosenheck/Elsie Larson; p. 237: Domino; p. 238: Domino (left), Sonya Yruel Photography/ Christina Vo of Conscioustyle (right);

p. 239: Annie Schlechter (left), Sarah Elliott/Dekar Design (right); pp. 240–241: Amy Neunsinger; p. 242: Beth Kirby; p. 243 (from left): Annie Schlechter, Domino, Paul Costello; p. 244: Christina Holmes; p. 245 (clockwise from left): Mikkel Vang, Michael Wiltbank; p. 246: Bobby Fisher; p. 247: Michael Wilkbank/Timo Weiland; p. 248: Nicole Franzen (left), Alpha Smoot (right); p. 249: Nicole Franzen (top), Chloe Crespi (middle), Winnie Au (bottom)

ADDITIONAL TEXT CREDITS

Amelia Fleetwood:

p. 39; pp. 44–45; pp. 74–75; pp. 100–101; pp. 130–131; p. 150; pp. 158–159; pp. 180–181; pp. 202–203; p. 221; pp. 224–225; p. 247; pp. 248–249

Alex Redgrave:

pp. 250–260

The authors would like to thank:
Jen Anderson, Kate Berry, Monika Eyers, Stephanie Harth, Anna Kocharian,
Meghan McNeer, Elaina Sullivan, Lily Sullivan, and Michael Wiltbank.

Our team would like to extend our sincere thanks to the photographers and
homeowners featured in this book. We are inspired by your creativity and style
and are so grateful to share your work and spaces here.

This book was produced by

MELCHER
MEDIA

124 West 13th St., New York, NY 10011
www.melcher.com

President and CEO: Charles Melcher
Vice President and COO: Bonnie Eldon
Senior Editor/Producer: Lauren Nathan
Production Manager: Susan Lynch
Digital Producer: Shannon Fanuko
Editorial Assistant: Victoria Spencer

Melcher Media would like to thank:
Chika Azuma, Callie Barlow, Jess Bass, Emma Blackwood, Amelie Chernin, Karl Daum, Hannah B. Flicker,
Barbara Gogan, Kitt Harris, Luke Jarvis, Aaron Kenedi, Luisa Lizoain, Kaarina Mackenzie, John Morgan,
Jennifer S. Muller, Nola Romano, Laura Roumanos, Anthony Salazar, Rachel Schlotfeldt, Adiya Taylor,
Zoe Valella, Suchan Vodoor, Lee Wilcox, Megan Worman, and Katy Yudin.